Literacy

for Social Change

Literacy
for Social Change

Lynn R. Curtis

Foreword by Hanna Arlene Fingeret

New Readers Press • Syracuse, New York

ISBN 0-88336-557-X

New Readers Press
Publishing Division of Laubach Literacy International
Box 131, Syracuse, New York 13210

Printed in the United States of America

Editorial assistant: Veronica Echenique
Designer: Patti DiCarlo

Photos of Bangladesh, Haiti, India, Mexico, Nepal, Philippines by Lynn Curtis, unless otherwise credited.

9 8 7 6 5 4 3 2 1

To the women and men whose struggles and triumphs shaped this volume

As an educator you are involved in social intervention. Your role is neither neutral nor passive. You either intervene on behalf of change or you intervene to prevent change.

Robert F. Caswell

Contents

Foreword

A group of women sat around a wobbly metal table in the "community room" of an inner-city housing project, talking about how angry they were at the condition of their building. They wanted to do something to change their living conditions. Slowly, they came to a decision as a group—they would write to City Hall. But they needed help reading and writing.

This was my introduction to adult literacy education. At that time it never occurred to me that there was any separation between learning and doing, between literacy and social action. It made sense to me that these women wanted to change their conditions, and developing literacy skills was simply one strategy toward that end. Our work together focused on their letters to City Hall rather than on the letters of the alphabet, but by the time they finished their correspondence with the city, every one of these women knew the alphabet and much, much more. They understood how those letters, when combined in certain ways, could be tools for changing the circumstances of their lives.

Because of this and similar experiences, I never had any question as to whether literacy education is political activity; it never was an intellectual debate for me, or an abstract notion. My knowledge was generated by my concrete experience; I was privileged to be part of the process through which these women and other adults came to know and use their power to bring about social change.

Since that time I have learned that this link between literacy and social action is not to be taken for granted. Indeed, the prevailing model of literacy education in the United States and many other industrialized nations is very individually oriented. Literacy is connected to individual change; it is a means of "getting ahead" and a route to personal betterment and individual social and economic mobility. Literacy is a key to a better job and a higher standard of living. The need for literacy skill development is considered a personal problem that hinders assimilation into the mainstream of society. This model of literacy education usually serves to promote the status quo.

In many other settings, however, literacy education is far more oriented to serving communities and to effecting social change. In literacy programs all over the world, educators and learners work together as advocates to transform the underlying conditions supporting poverty and the lack of early schooling. In these programs, literacy education is understood in the context of adults' lives rather than separated from it. That context—the community's issues, problems, aspirations, skills, cultures, languages—creates the basis for literacy work as well as the tools to engage in it.

Literacy programs oriented to social change often address other social issues as well, such as poverty, homelessness, civil rights, and women's equity. As participants are moved to action, they threaten the status quo—such is the nature of change. Resistance often develops, either overtly or covertly. However, in spite of the obstacles that often are thrown in their paths, many courageous adults continue to come together in literacy programs for positive social change. In this book, Lynn Curtis draws pictures for us of literacy practices across the globe that are dedicated to promoting equality and justice. In these programs, the participants use literacy skills to address economic, social, and political issues and thereby challenge the structures that support the continuing illiteracy in their societies. In the process, the participants become literate about their world as well as the word, and use their understanding to inform their action.

The four elements presented in this book—fundamental skills, critical thinking, culture, and group action—support a process through which learners develop a critical perspective on the social structures within which they live. Learners also act on their analysis as a group to improve their lives. These elements are deceptively simple. They place at the center of literacy education that which has meaning to learners. But meaning is a very complex thing, connected at its core to culture, experience, and language. Meaning changes as adults change; as we expand our experience we reconstruct the meaning of texts. And as we read and write more, we increase our capacity to engage in meaningful social change. Curtis helps us understand how to channel our literacy efforts so that we serve larger goals of constructive community and societal change rather than simply serving to promote the status quo. He reminds us that such programs must be dynamic; as participants change and the social conditions change, the programs that serve learners must change as well.

Curtis's work has a clear philosophical rationale, and is consistent with the implications of recent cognitive science research findings as well. We are learning that cognitive development is the result of interaction between a person's unique characteristics (biological, intellectual, physiological, emotional, and so on) and that person's social context. When literacy development occurs in the family or neighborhood, it increases everyone's chances of being successful. We also know that learning is facilitated when new concepts are connected to concepts that have already been learned. And we understand that adults will most easily be able to use their new skills when there is a relationship between the processes used to develop those skills and the processes needed to apply them. In other words, learning and using new skills are facilitated when instruction includes meaningful and relevant content and tasks. Improving the conditions of their lives is an extremely meaningful task for adults in the programs Curtis describes.

Literacy is a right rather than a privilege today. Effective literacy programs can take many forms, but all are rooted in a fundamental respect for learners—their culture, their experience, and their aspirations. This requires that literacy learners and educators work together as partners, understanding that each brings a type of expertise necessary for success. Old roles of students-waiting-to-be-told and teachers-endowing-students-with-knowledge have to be transformed; old relationships between experts and learners have to be reshaped. Most important, old stereotypes of nonreaders as incompetent "blank slates" must be shattered and replaced by a more complex, respectful understanding of the dignity and the power nonreading adults bring to their participation in literacy instruction.

Lynn Curtis has provided us with some important tools. We could simply read this book as an interesting description of one genre of literacy practice. Or we can rise to his challenge to move to action and use our literacy skills to work together to create a better world for us all.

Hanna Arlene Fingeret
Raleigh, NC
March, 1990

Acknowledgments

For inspiration and collaboration, thanks to Robert Caswell, Dr. Luís Oscar Londoño, Guillermina López Bravo, Muriel Medina, Linda Church, Raúl Añorve, Karen Kaye, Louis Ste. Marie, Hanna Arlene Fingeret, Paul Jurmo, David Werner, Kathleen Kelly, Lucille Watahomigie, California Literacy, Inc., and Laubach Literacy International. For editorial insight and extraordinary patience, a special thank you to Teddy Kempster. And for love and long suffering, thanks to Sandy, David, Bret, Chad, Lyndee, Kimberlee, and Kristee.

This publication was made possible through the generous financial help of:

The Chase Manhattan Foundation
The Irvine Foundation
The Ahmanson Foundation
and
Amelia A. Rankin

Part I

Definitions and Model: Literacy for Social Change

Chapter 1

What is literacy?

Not long ago, scholars, planners, and practitioners gathered at a conference entitled "The Definition of Literacy." For days they debated one question, "What is literacy?" They couldn't agree on the answer. The controversy wasn't a squabble over technicalities. In the literacy debate, stakes are high. At risk are public policies, money, and human lives—all over the meaning of one word.

Debates such as this one rage long and furious. Everyone agrees that literacy has to do with some body of skills or understanding regarded as fundamental and essential. Most definitions include reading and writing in the list of basics, but the nature and level of proficiency in reading and writing are often controversial matters. Is it enough to be able to decode simple written words or to fill out forms? Should the definition of literacy include the ability to comprehend and critically question written language as well as to use it to analyze and solve problems?

The literacy argument extends beyond the debate about written communication. What listening, speaking, and computation skills should or shouldn't be included in the definition of literacy? Some maintain that literacy is the ability to read, and that reading is the pivotal, central skill around which all others revolve. This argument suggests that the more advanced one's reading capacities, then, by definition, the more advanced are one's abilities to analyze and apply knowledge. Learning to read would therefore involve a wide range of skills, and in this sense truly being able to read would be synonymous with being "educated." A slightly different notion suggests that reading is on an equal footing with other communication skills and that literacy is the integration of many skills, including reading.

Others argue that the actual skill levels attained are less important than the cultural, social, or political context in which skills are developed. A hotter argument focuses on who—the learners, teachers, or particular institutions—defines literacy's fundamental body of learning and why the decision makers view certain skills or insights as essential.

These concerns involve much more than a contest over semantics and theory. To define literacy is to state social values. The definition, whatever it is, reflects basic assumptions about the nature and function of education in society.

How crucial is the definition? Consider the groups of people who have the greatest need for literacy programs—the poor and disenfranchised. In the United States, for example, virtually every measure indicates that among African-Americans, Hispanics, and Native Americans, the illiteracy rates are double or triple those of whites. Illiteracy is not the cause of poverty, but is inextricably tied to it and to the social ills of racism and inequality. Literacy is one starting point for dealing with these social problems. Resources need to be targeted where the need is most intense—among minority and marginalized population groups. This requires a working definition of literacy sufficient to meet the unique needs of these groups.

Those who face the greatest need for learning are those who have the least opportunity to get it, or are least likely to show any interest—partly because they have the least say in shaping answers to the questions just posed. All too often, literacy programs in the inner city, the reservation, the *barrio*, or remote rural areas are underfunded or simply don't exist. And when the programs in these areas are established, they frequently don't incorporate the leadership, community issues, and cultural strengths of the people for whom the program was intended. The results are disappointing.

Many exemplary literacy programs seek a broader vision of literacy so that they might more effectively serve those currently underserved population groups. For those, and for any who want to better understand the issues involved, the following cases illustrate the range of meanings that individuals and institutions attach to the concept of literacy.

Literacy and community change

Bangladesh, Comilla region

Twenty impoverished women of the same rural village, some holding infant children, crowded on the dirt floor of a two-room hut. They were participating in a beginning literacy class. Fastened to the mud wall was a simple printed poster depicting a rural woman seated on the ground. The woman rested her forehead on her hand while tears flowed down her anguished face. She was surrounded by five small children, three of whom were naked. They were all crying, obviously for food because the seated young ones held empty plates. The children were skeleton-skinny, with the bloated stomachs of malnutrition. Under the bitter scene was one word printed in Bengali, the language of the participants. The word was *hunger.*

Courtesy Bangladesh Rural Advancement Committee

The women in the room reacted emotionally to the picture. Many were living through the experiences reflected in the face of the crying woman. These women had known first-hand the killer cyclones that left widows and orphans in their village, the floods that left starvation harvests, and the helplessness of hungry children. Although few of the women had ever before read the written word *hunger,* it became a permanent new entry in their small, but growing, reading vocabulary. They wrote the word and learned some of its component sounds. They began to internalize the profound discovery that written words could symbolize meaningful realities in their lives.

This was much more than a motivational vocabulary or phonics lesson. The mechanics of reading were almost incidental to the discussion about the scene and the feelings depicted in the poster. The leader, a village woman named Noli who read at a level slightly higher than the students, joined the lively but informal dialogue.

The women talked of their own experiences of pain and frustration as mothers. They talked about their poverty and the problems they experienced on a daily basis. They chose to discuss this theme for many days. They learned a few more sounds and symbols in the process, and identified problems in their lives, the causes of those problems, and some possible solutions. They took action as a group to begin addressing these problems through self-initiated projects including a cooperative garden and a project to make and sell woven goods.

For these women, literacy meant skills in listening, speaking, math, needs assessment, goal setting, group dynamics, politics, culture, and history. To be sure, fundamental reading and writing skills had an important place. In five years, all the women improved their reading skills to varying degrees. Only 20 percent, however, attained what would be regarded as a seventh-grade reading level in the United States.

Many wonderful and permanent changes in the lives of these women and their community have resulted. New and lasting patterns of mutual support and action have emerged. All participants have attained new skills and attitudes to define and solve individual and collective problems. By their own unique but ambitious standards, they have become far more "educated."

Literacy and reading and writing fundamentals

Provo, Utah

An unemployed steel worker, a young mother who is the volunteer leader of a church youth program, a high school custodian, a construction supervisor, and a recent high school graduate—these typify the people enrolled at Project Read, the public library adult literacy program. Extremely embarrassed about their limited reading skills, they have attempted to keep their "illiteracy" a secret. They each receive one-to-one tutoring from a volunteer trained in the methods used by Laubach Literacy Action or Literacy Volunteers of America.

Many of the learners identify with the values of a middle-class lifestyle; some enjoy such a lifestyle already. They view their reading limitations as a humiliating impediment to that lifestyle and seek to hide and ultimately overcome their "deficiency." For them, a direct personal or financial payoff is associated with learning to read. For the most part, they are highly motivated to complete the program.

Such motivation, including the courage to seek help on their own, prompts many authors to refer to this type of student as the "cream" of America's massive nonreading crop. For tutors and students alike, the learning experience is highly rewarding. Students meet privately with tutors, who are for the most part white and middle class, once or twice a week for an hour or two each session. A majority of them complete the tutoring program in about eighteen months and advance to a reading level equivalent to the sixth or seventh grade. Through this experience, learners gain fundamental reading and writing skills. They master many skills in comprehension and establish a solid base for further learning.

At this point, learners are regarded as having achieved literacy. Some go on to further education and/or job training. Many speak of their learning experience as a turning point in their lives, the beginning of a marvelous individual transformation made possible by the new skills and confidence they once thought unattainable.

A tutor and student work together on basic reading skills. Volunteer tutor organizations are active in communities throughout the United States. Anthony Potter Photography

Literacy and the revolution

Nicaragua

A rooster's crow awakened Enrique. The sixteen-year-old high school student from distant Managua arose from a sleeping mat on a hard floor. This teenager from the city would share the day's hard field labor and meager food of his host family and then conduct a literacy-learning session with them. That evening the Archuleta family, who had housed their youthful instructor for several weeks, would learn some new reading vocabulary while discussing the impact of Nicaragua's revolution on their own family income.

For Enrique, the experience was a painful yet rewarding learning process. It was his first encounter with Nicaragua's rural poverty, an opportunity to be part of a compelling national movement, and a chance to share in the learning of others. For the Archuletas and their neighbors, who housed other youthful volunteers, the experience was their introduction to the revolution and their first exposure to formal education.

Enrique was only one of an army of fervent high school youth—*brigadistas*—who traveled throughout the countryside of Nicaragua to spread the *Sandinista* vision of literacy. The ambitious campaign matched trained though inexperienced volunteers with rural families throughout the nation and aimed for mass basic education over a limited time period.

All of the thousands of volunteers used the same materials. Without question, one purpose of the campaign was to enable nonreaders to gain specific reading and writing skills. But the main focus of the effort was to engage participants in dialogue regarding social, economic, and political issues in their lives. As the campaign leaders clearly declared, the primary purpose was to advance the aspirations of the revolution "and also teach them to read."

Critics of the campaign charge that the effort was primarily an exploitative propaganda move on behalf of the new government's agenda. They describe it as a maneuver to consolidate the *Sandinistas'* base of power. Supporters describe the enthusiastic involvement of previously illiterate peasants in empowering dialogue about the issues and concerns of their lives. They suggest that all literacy education is actually based on ideology, even if that ideology isn't explicitly stated. They argue that the *Sandinistas* are simply more candid than others about the purposes of their literacy program.

Regardless of the controversy, none can deny that the effort was a logistical triumph, with large numbers of impoverished people accomplishing an overwhelming task.

Literacy and development

Philippines, near Cavite

Landless farm workers were celebrating a proud achievement. They had completed one of their mutual goals, a squatter toilet that flushes when one pours water in it. It was the first toilet in their *barangay* (neighborhood). Many more would follow.

Six months earlier, they had met with a facilitator from the Philippine Rural Reconstruction Movement. Together they developed a plan to address many of their perceived community needs. The facilitator also proposed a literacy program to complement their grassroots development effort. Some showed interest, and weekly classes began. The participants learned Tagalog language basics from structured materials that present a sequential series of reading skills. But the learners soon became restless. They worked long hours daily to eke out a survival income, and already were devoting hours of their remaining time to the participatory community development process. The literacy classes seemed unconnected to activities that were far more relevant to their felt needs. A technically superb reading program soon proved boring and irrelevant, and the classes were dropped.

Concerned community organizers who developed the literacy program remain perplexed. They wonder if reading education could somehow become more vitally connected to the participatory problem-solving process in which villagers are so actively involved. Could reading and writing instruction integrated with the development process actually enhance the success of both efforts? They think so, but they aren't quite sure how to make it happen. They're struggling to find a broader and more relevant definition of literacy.

Literacy and social/political awareness

San Francisco

In San Francisco's inner-city Mission District, African-Americans, Hispanics, and Southeast Asians account for most of the population. Members of these different groups rarely cross racial lines except to conduct routine business or perhaps to fight. These groups feel isolated not only from each other, but from the broader community as well.

Project Literacy, a neighborhood nonprofit organization, was formed to counteract this sense of isolation and alienation. Michael James, one of the project's several coordinators, observed, "People living under oppressed conditions are made to feel as though their neighbors—other oppressed people—are the enemy, when really they are all victims of the same oppression. If they remain divided, they can do nothing about the problem."

In the late seventies and early eighties, Project Literacy organized several small, multi-ethnic groups of young adults. Many of the participants had limited reading skills, but they didn't come to learn basic "reading." The focus of their literacy experience was not the acquisition of fundamental reading and writing skills. No one bore the title "teacher." All were regarded as co-learners, not in a school class taught by an expert, but in a learning circle of equals.

Together they examined the realities and problems of their own lives with an emphasis on the broader social, political, and economic roots of these problems. Brazilian educator Paulo Freire's problem-posing praxis, which is a format for analyzing learner-identified problems, causes, effects, and possible solutions, provided the basis for group dialogue. A central text for discussion was Freire's *Pedagogy of the Oppressed.*

Many learning activities helped improve reading and writing skills. Sometimes one learner tutored another who needed help with specific fundamental reading skills, but the group focus was on the broader issues of the learners' lives and the relationship of education and social action to those issues. Many of the "graduates" of this experience have returned to become organizers and "co-coordinators" of subsequent learning circles. In this project, literacy has a meaning far beyond fundamental reading skills.

An alternative model

The examples just described reflect just a few of the prevailing concepts of literacy. Some others include English for speakers of other languages, workplace literacy (which emphasizes both basic and job-related skills), and cultural literacy (which involves knowledge of "essential" cultural and historic facts).

Illiteracy is tied to poverty, racism, and other social ills whether in the United States, *above,* or in developing nations such as India, *below.*

Many proponents of these various visions of literacy are highly critical of those who hold a different point of view. Yet in reality, they have more in common with each other than they may realize. They have much to share in support of each other.

In the following chapter, I introduce a model of literacy education that integrates the best of these many different perspectives. I am not the author of this model, but I have observed it in practice. This model is in many ways an ideal, but it is far more than theoretical. It is an attainable standard that has emerged from decades of field experience among impoverished learners, and at the very least, it is a mirror of possibilities that might occur if programs examine their assumptions honestly and critically. Most importantly, this model is based upon a definition of literacy strong enough to create the changes necessary for a just and equitable society. It is a powerful alternative for effectively addressing the literacy needs of the hundreds of millions of adults from the ranks of the poor and oppressed who remain unserved by existing education and development opportunities.

The sheer size of this unserved and marginalized population suggests how important the integrative model might be. In the United States alone, the most conservative statistics indicate that a minimum of twenty-three million adults are literacy deficient, and this number is growing. All adult literacy programs presently conducted by public schools, industry, government, prisons, libraries, foundations, volunteer organizations, adult basic education, and special interest groups combined involve no more than 10 percent of these adults. For the 90 percent of literacy-deficient individuals for whom there are no programs, alternative approaches are desperately needed.

Worldwide, the problem is even worse. Nine hundred million adults have no opportunity to obtain the listening, speaking, reading, writing, and math skills they need to meet basic human needs and participate actively in the development and transformation of their communities. Their lack of access to new information, skills, and insights ensures that they remain trapped in poverty and in social, economic, and political disenfranchisement. Violence, misery, crime, and political turmoil are the prices they and society at large continue to pay for this inequality.

There is urgent need for a literacy alternative with the strength to confront this disturbing reality.

Chapter 2

A vision and a model

In 1977, representatives of Colombian *campesino* groups gathered for an extraordinary meeting. Each delegate represented a village-level initiative that was successfully combining literacy and community action. Each group's literacy effort had been supported by tiny grants and technical assistance from Laubach Literacy International. In this gathering, they met each other for the first time and realized that other villages suffered the same impoverished conditions, and in many cases were working toward similar solutions. Although the villages were experiencing very similar problems and successes, they were isolated from each other and previously unaware of the experiences of others like themselves.

In each village, the people had learned to read and write within the context of their own community issues. Learners had gained fundamental listening, speaking, reading, writing, and math skills, while learning had focused on the cultural, social, economic, and political realities of their daily life experience. As they learned fundamental skills, they talked about these realities. They identified the problems of their tiny community, determined the causes of these problems, proposed solutions, and organized for action. They had begun a number of projects to address their problems, including cooperatives, community gardens, income-generation projects, and health initiatives. They had also begun several activities aimed at creating solidarity and a shared sense of esteem and pride through cultural expression. Through song, skit, and history, they celebrated the strengths of their community.

Delegates from the villages discussed the shared realities of poverty and powerlessness that characterized their communities. And they spoke of the changes their villages were making in response to the challenge.

As they spoke of mutual challenges, they also began to articulate a compelling shared vision of a world for which they are working. Their local successes had given them a glimpse of a possible way of life that had once been beyond their imagination. They spoke enthusiastically and positively about the "new society" they were building through their literacy programs.

Robert F. Caswell, president of Laubach Literacy International and an observer at these meetings, described the grassroots vision this way: "Their 'new society' has no prototype. It is not modeled on Soviet Russia; it is not a communist society. It is not modeled after the United States; it is not a capitalist society. It is neither a Cuba, nor a China, nor a Nicaragua. People were not talking about a political system. Instead, they described in simple terms a society that meets their basic needs for food, housing, clothing, and health care. They talked about a society that would give them the dignity of work—a labor-intensive society that meets the needs of the many, rather than a technology-dependent society producing manufactured goods for a few."

These learners were describing the way they believe people ought to live and deal with one another. Their vision concerns changes of heart and attitude leading to a more just economic and social order. They believe their literacy efforts help them to move closer to their vision.

Caswell later linked this vision to Laubach Literacy International's commitment to worldwide literacy efforts. In his words, "We are so committed because we believe that literate people are essential to realizing the vision of a just and peaceful world community, a world community characterized by freedom of opportunity, the equitable distribution of natural resources, and public and private actions to attain food, clothing, shelter, employment, health care, education, and spiritual nurturing for all."

A definition to match the vision

Is such a society possible? Absolutely—but not when large numbers of people lack control over the language of their lives. No matter how equitable the political and economic structure, no matter how enlightened the leadership or fair the distribution of income, those who don't have control over the language are controlled by those who do. Governments may change. But one form of dictatorship is replaced by another when people don't have access to the information that influences their lives.

Literacy can bring each citizen and community of citizens the power to shape their society.

For an empowered citizenry to take its full and essential role, a definition of literacy bold enough to match the compelling vision of a "new society" is required. The mission statement of Laubach Literacy International offers such a definition. It defines literacy as "the listening, speaking, reading, writing, and mathematics skills adults and older youth need to solve the problems they encounter in daily life; to take full advantage of opportunities in their environment; and to participate fully in the transformation of their society."

This definition is bold enough to generate the "new society" that people are seeking. For those who are poor and marginalized, such a definition is essential. It shapes an attainable and realistic model for practice. Through decades of experimentation, a number of groups have tested and successfully applied this model, which I will call "literacy for social change." It includes concepts typically associated with the term "popular education," but also involves activities connected with community development and even traditional education.

In its ideal form, literacy for social change integrates learning and community change. The model addresses listening, speaking, reading, writing, and math skills as well as new attitudes and consciousness, and has the following four interrelated components:

- fundamental skills
- critical thinking
- cultural expression
- individual/community action

Fundamental skills

Fundamental skills are the basic skills necessary for dealing with the written word. Fundamental reading skills enable a person to decode written words, and usually include the development of a basic sight vocabulary, and an understanding of phonics and certain elements of grammar and punctuation. Such skills are finite and measurable.

The term is often extended to include writing, listening, speaking, and math. In the areas of listening and speaking, particularly with regard to learning a second language, these skills are often referred to as survival skills.

In the United States, the term "illiteracy" usually refers to gaps in one or more of these fundamental skills. One point of view holds that fundamental skill instruction requires a systematic effort to identify and fill all the gaps and build a solid, sequential skill foundation for further learning. Another view insists that highly motivated learners in the right environment will acquire the missing skills as a by-product of a learning process focused on gaining meaning rather than individual skills.

In the literacy debate, few argue against the value of fundamental skills. The controversy generally centers around the content of words and ideas selected for instruction, the method of instruction, the extent to which learning fundamental skills is linked with other learning and action goals, and the degree to which sociopolitical consciousness is a recognized goal of the process.

Critical thinking

Fundamental skills are necessary but insufficient tools for fully controlling written language. Critical thinking includes the capacity to understand and react to information. Learners who develop critical thinking skills not only understand the meaning of what they hear and read, but question its content, seek additional information, and synthesize information to identify and analyze the problems they encounter in daily life, the causes of these problems, and alternatives for action.

These learners are not passive recipients of knowledge or experience. They question, analyze, and reflect upon what they hear, read, and experience. They are able to draw inferences, recognize implied meaning, distinguish between fact and opinion, consider opposing positions, and synthesize information to make it applicable to their unique circumstances. In speech and writing, they express their conclusions and solutions.

All citizens need critical thinking skills, but for learners among marginalized, poorer populations, one aspect of these skills is essential. For these groups to confront their overwhelming conditions of poverty, they need to be conscious of the forces and societal structures that cause their powerlessness. Critically conscious, they become aware of tremendous social changes necessary to transform their own communities and the larger society. Their literacy learning makes it possible for them to pursue both individual and community change.

It is sometimes argued that critical thinking, in a perfect sense, is a lifetime pursuit fully achieved only by a select few with advanced and formal education. But the point is debatable, and not relevant here. Most of the skills and attitudes associated with the term critical thinking are realistically attainable by all—not just a few intellectuals. It's admirable that an elite percentage are able to refine their intellectual skills to high levels of critical thinking. But given the right learning opportunities, the essential critical thinking skills are within the reach of the majority of people.

Cultural expression

Much of what is real and important for literacy learners, indeed for all people, is experienced on an emotional or spiritual level. The most important realities of individual and community life—the joys and yearnings, struggles and achievements—must be understood, shared, and celebrated. Yet conventional forms of speech or writing are often inadequate to express these realities. Music, drama, folklore, dance, literature, and art are frequently better suited. When the literacy program includes cultural expression as a fundamental component, learners feel their worth as individuals and communities.

Cultural expression as an integral part of literacy learning is particularly essential among disenfranchised population groups. It helps them develop strengths to resist the ongoing barrage against their own sense of worth. Minority learners have generally endured a lifetime of assault on their culture. Through mainstream education, the media, and other institutions that control their lives, they have been taught the degrading message that their culture is inferior to that of the dominant society. Learners from such groups often doubt the worth of themselves, their families, and their communities. Far from frivolous or romantic, cultural expression is frequently the most potent medium for generating societal change and enabling full participation in the life of one's community. It is both a means and an end with regard to learning and development.

Varying levels of listening, speaking, reading, writing, or math skills, as well as sensitivity, are needed to convey cultural experience. These skill levels are tangible and distinct, but not quite so readily quantifiable as fundamental skills. The capacity to appreciate or write a poem that truly expresses inner feelings involves much more than the mere mechanics of meter and verse.

Action

"Actions speak louder than words." The familiar adage has profound implications for literacy education. While learners may successfully express and reflect upon problems and successes in their lives, their capacity to learn and bring about change remains limited until they act upon their concerns.

Literacy education is complete only when specific actions are taken to address issues arising through the learning process. Through action, learning is not only reinforced, it is fulfilled.

Critics of deliberate action projects in literacy education suggest that such steps divert learners from more important objectives. They argue that impoverished learners take action steps that only fit within their limited skill and resource range. Tremendous energy devoted to planting a better garden or digging a well diverts the participants' energy and focus from global causes and solutions to the problems they face. They maintain that such steps may fulfill the learners' urge to do something, but draw attention away from more profound needs and possibilities.

This argument is flawed. Critical consciousness of broader issues without a self-directed capacity to act leaves learners aware, but still powerless. They remain dependent upon someone else's direction before they can act. If people don't develop the capacity to act for change, even if that action begins with humble measures, others will continue to act for and upon them. Consciousness of causal issues should be combined with specific action projects. The two can be effectively integrated. In action projects, learners have the opportunity to apply listening, speaking, reading, writing, and math skills to real-life activities. All the skills learned take on a new relevance when put to the test through application.

Fitting the pieces together

This literacy model is greater than the sum of its parts. Its success depends not only upon the learners achieving goals in the separate areas of fundamental skills, critical thinking, cultural expression, and action steps, but also in realizing these achievements in an integrated way. Many practitioners and theorists, including the renowned educator Paulo Freire, effectively advocate individual components of this model. Numerous books and articles explore in detail the fundamental skills of reading or advocate education for liberation through critical thinking and consciousness raising. Many of these studies are excellent, but few of them combine all four areas in a way that is readily accessible to practitioners. That is the unique contribution of the literacy-for-social-change model.

While participants learn fundamental skills, reading, writing, and discussions are focused on activities that generate critical awareness of the realities that affect their lives. This learning is combined with opportunities for cultural expression and learner-initiated action projects.

This integrative process takes time. But as the process continues, evidence of lasting community change becomes apparent. Learners begin to build their "new society." So conceived, literacy isn't something separate from individual and community development. It is the necessary first step in the process of personal, socioeconomic, and political change.

The literacy-for-social-change model is more than a good idea. It works. I've seen its power reflected in the faces of thousands of determined men and women who are indeed transforming their communities. With limited support from Laubach Literacy International, a number of grassroots groups continue to discover their own potential.

The model has evolved from decades of field experience that started with the catalytic efforts of literacy leader Frank C. Laubach in the 1950s. During the sixties and seventies, grassroots groups in Colombia developed the model with the pioneering contributions of educators Dr. Luís Oscar Londoño and Robert F. Caswell. The model continues to evolve today in Latin America, Asia, Africa, the Middle East, and the United States. Two exemplary programs, located in Colombia and Mexico, illustrate the potential for learner-initiated change that emerges from this approach.

Life in a burning garbage dump

When I first saw Medellín's garbage dump, the *Basurero*, in 1982, it looked like a giant smoldering ant hill. The 400-foot-high mountain of burning garbage in Colombia's largest city teemed with the thirty thousand people who made their home there.

In the midst of stench, smoke, and filth, thousands who fled the poverty and starvation of the countryside lived in shacks made of trash. They had no income for rent; they were squatters on the land that was Medellín's municipal garbage dump. *Basurero* dwellers had no public facilities for water, electricity, or sewage. Few had access to paying jobs. And all competed with large black buzzards for *chute*, their term for food, picked from the simmering refuse heap. Toddlers crawled in the filth, and thousands of men, women, and children labored all day scavenging acres of smoking trash for bottles, clothes, cans, and metal to sell for pennies.

A year earlier, many residents of one section of the *Basurero* had gathered to see if they could do something to improve their desperate conditions. Few of them could read or write, and they had little idea where they could begin. They elected leaders, who in turn sought assistance from the Laubach Center for Adult Basic Education in Medellín. The leaders identified simple key words and phrases having personal significance to the people—words like *garbage, health, food,* and *fire.* Volunteers from within the garbage dump then taught their neighbors to read these and other words they had identified as important.

As participants learned to read, they discussed the reality of the key words. They considered local, national, and international causes of the problems they faced. They analyzed historical, current, and future implications. For the first time, these learners began to talk about solutions to problems they once thought unsolvable. In this one *barrio,* there was concrete evidence of the impact of their literacy experience. Participants proudly displayed projects to introduce electricity, sewage disposal, and homes of brick instead of trash. A new sense of community was emerging, but at the same time in neighboring *barrios,* isolated, hopeless individuals struggled alone.

Friendship and solidarity were evident among the impoverished residents of this particular *barrio,* while hostility and alienation coexisted in the adjacent *barrios.* These neighborhoods had no comparable plans for change or improvement.

The garbage dump in Medellín was considered a virtual war zone of crime, violence, and despair. The lone exception was the *barrio* that participated in the literacy learning process. It had become a kind of hopeful island. In February 1982, however, the newly developing problem-solving skills of the people in the Laubach program were put to a grim test. Heat from the smoldering garbage mountain ignited a wildfire. Before the blaze was doused, sixty homes were destroyed. Miraculously, no one was injured, but the added misery of sixty families left homeless and without possessions appeared unbearable.

The day after the fire, witnesses wept, not for the tragedy, but for the unexpected triumph. Two of the literacy leaders, Augusto and José, showed visitors the charred site where scores of surprisingly enthusiastic people were laboring.

Within hours after the fire, the literacy groups had organized themselves for action. There would be no government disaster relief, but few mourned the loss of their shacks. With sweat, shovels, and strings for measuring, they celebrated the opportunity to build new and better homes. From ashes came moving victory. Although they still faced horrendous problems, these people of the *Basurero* were discovering new skills and demonstrating concrete hope for the future.

Desolation and filth characterize living conditions for residents of the *Basurero* in Medellín, Colombia.

Since the fire, the city has stopped dumping garbage in the *Basurero*, and the people have gradually improved conditions in their area. Now they have electricity, running water, improved drainage, cooperative income-generating projects, a clinic and community center, and homes of brick. As their property has become more valuable, unscrupulous developers have tried to take their land away by saying that the residents have no legal claim to it. Those involved in the literacy process were able to write a history of their *barrio* which provided the legal evidence needed to keep their land.

Many more *barrios* in the *Basurero* have since become involved in the literacy-for-social-change process. Through learning and community action, these neighborhoods have organized themselves to generate income, provide basic health and educational services, and complete extensive home building and improvement. In fact, the model has been successfully applied by Laubach-supported groups in fifty-seven other impoverished urban *barrios* and rural villages throughout Colombia and also in Bolivia.

Though each of these many participating sites deals with slightly different underlying concerns, the integrated literacy process has enabled participants to realize changes similar to those experienced in the *Basurero*. Mountain coffee workers, destitute fishing families, urban slum dwellers struggling to survive Medellín's drug violence, and other Colombian village and *barrio* populations have used literacy for social change to confront the realities of poverty and create lasting solutions.

Literacy for social change has transformed neighborhoods in the *Basurero* and other communities throughout Colombia.

A fever for learning

Two hundred miles north of Mexico City, a parched, dusty road leads to the remote *rancho* (small village) of Tinaja de Negrete. Here are tree-tall cactus, small adobe homes, and fields of dry maize and sorghum. Tinaja is the center of fourteen *ranchos* where some twenty-five hundred *campesino* families scrape a bare living from the hot ground.

Baked by the desert sun, the barren landscape of Tinaja holds treacherous health hazards for children and their parents. Leonora, a literacy learner, hugged her two young daughters as she spoke of the fever that had gripped her children at different times. They had been bitten by scorpions. Lurking in the rocks that are everywhere, scorpions strike often, and parents complained that the bites have been a frightening health danger.

Gastrointestinal problems were also common. Income and diets were inadequate, and poor nutrition caused sickness. Tinaja had no well. A rain reservoir that had become brackish and stagnant in the dry season was the only source of drinking water. Doctors rarely made the bumpy ride to Tinaja. Even if they did, people had no money to pay medical bills. The people of Tinaja had identified health issues as their highest priority, and the literacy classes reflected this concern. Words like *water*

In the literacy-for-social-change process, learning is linked to local needs; in Tinaja, Mexico, these needs are captured in the key words *agua* and *medicina.*

and *medicine* have introduced health concepts to generate discussion and group action. The people have further emphasized health and nutrition education through puppet theater, skits, and music.

As a result of this Laubach program, the *ranchos* have acquired their own village medicine chests. Local paramedics and midwives have been trained. The people have repaired roads and negotiated a bus service. They have cleaned and repaired their homes, and built a small clinic for a visiting doctor. Nutrition and income have improved through cooperative poultry, gardening, and livestock projects. They raise and harvest fish for sale and consumption through ambitious aquaculture fish ponds. All of these efforts came from local initiative. They emerged from the literacy-for-social-change process.

Literacy has also helped bring water from the ground. New skills and confidence gained through the literacy learning experience inspired the learners of Tinaja to approach the regional government for help to drill a well. The government office covered 90 percent of the cost of a new well, and today residents enjoy running water and electricity.

The success of this literacy effort has spread from Tinaja to twenty-two neighboring *ranchos*. Other central Mexican communities, some a great distance from these *ranchos*, are also following Tinaja's example to form similar literacy action efforts.

Powerful learning

The remarkable individual and community transformations realized through Laubach literacy-for-social-change projects in Mexico and Colombia are not unusual nor are they unique to Latin America. They are examples of an education and action model applicable to any cultural or geographic setting, especially among poor, marginalized populations. In the inner-city streets of Chicago, the alleyways of London's minority districts, or the rural paths of Mandalay, literacy for social change offers a pattern for hope and improvement.

When disenfranchised people gather to learn and act in an effort that integrates the development of fundamental skills, critical thinking, cultural expression, and action, dramatic, positive changes are the norm. For example, in Thailand's northern San Kampaeng district, once destitute women are now generating income, improving their homes, and educating their children. Lower-caste families in the lowlands of Nepal's Chitwan district have planted forests, built a community center, established cooperative gardens, and improved family health. Inner-city residents of a poor Fort Lauderdale, Florida, neighborhood have organized community action initiatives based on neighborhood histories and cultural events. Desert villages in Sierra Leone are developing new income sources, sanitation and nutrition improvements, and health projects. The geography and languages vary. The cultures and climates are drastically different. But in each of these cases, the literacy-for-social-change experience results in powerful learning and lasting community development.

From Houston to Istanbul, from Guatemala City to Mombasa, the possibilities are universal. Literacy for social change offers a viable, nonviolent alternative for people anywhere who confront great social, economic, and political need. And for educators, leaders, and citizens who care about the future of our people and communities—both at home and worldwide—it is a model that offers a host of hopeful and creative new options.

Chapter 3

What is an effective literacy program?

By design, very few efforts that take on the title "literacy" try to include all four components of literacy for social change. This is not a veiled criticism, not an implication that these efforts are incomplete or ineffective. A program's effectiveness is measured in terms of the goals it sets.

Program effectiveness begins and ends not with administration or public relations or fund-raising, but with the people for whom the program really exists, the learners. The actual measure of a given program's effectiveness comes down to two questions. Is the learning program based on goals that come from the learners? Are learners experiencing success in an instructional process that moves them closer to their goals?

Why do adults enter literacy programs? Their reasons for enrollment—their goals—may be very simply to learn fundamental reading skills as quickly and efficiently as possible. Their goals may involve a spectrum of social, cultural, economic, and political implications. The learners' goals may be stated and clearly understood, or they may be unstated and not fully perceived. In any case, their stated and unstated motivations for participation are the foundation for an effective program. Learners will expend the necessary time and energy to participate if they experience success in an instructional process that moves them toward these goals.

This definition of effectiveness cuts through the controversy about how literacy should be defined and what a "good" literacy program is all about. Effective literacy programs enable learners to move toward their goals. Literacy programs focusing on any or all of the components described in the preceding chapter can be effective provided a) their efforts are based upon learner goals, and b) the learners experience success in the instructional process.

Not every practitioner and theorist shares this perspective. Many insist that there is one "right" kind of literacy program. Leaders sometimes take a moralistic position and criticize the work of otherwise effective programs because they concentrate on goals different from their own. In fact, a great deal of the time and resources that could be focused on needed literacy education gets lost in heated but misplaced criticism.

The five educational programs described in chapter 1 mirror the range of meanings attached to the concept of literacy. None of the programs integrate all four components of the literacy-for-social-change model. Are they to be judged as misguided or incomplete? Let's take a second look at these five programs, along with some of the common criticisms made about each of them or their type of program. If they are judged in light of how they help learners meet their goals, they can be recognized for their genuine contribution and potential.

Literacy and community change

Bangladesh, Comilla region

Twenty percent of the impoverished participants of this women's program mastered fundamental reading skills. All the women gained confidence and capacity in the other fundamental skills of listening, speaking, and math sufficient to initiate several community development projects, cultural events, and political action steps. The participatory process enabled once submissive, victimized women to become socially and politically conscious and active. All learners developed a deeper appreciation of the power of the written word, and one-fifth of the learners gained solid proficiency in basic reading and writing skills.

Common criticism: The program failed. Only 20 percent learned the fundamentals of reading and writing. Their other achievements are built upon a shaky foundation that won't sustain future learning. There are gaps in the basic reading and writing skills of 80 percent of the women. Until those gaps are filled, the participants will remain controlled by those who have mastered the written word.

Women in this Bangladesh literacy class develop confidence in their problem-solving abilities while learning fundamental reading skills. Bangladesh Literacy Society

Another view: The program was effective. Women who had never experienced formal education discovered that learning is connected to their ability to solve problems. They identified problems in their environment and solved them. They met their learning goals and experienced success in the instructional process.

Increasing proficiency in reading and writing was not their highest priority. Yet they all developed some reading skills. Nearly all the learners also improved their listening, speaking, and math skills. They all gained greater control over the language of their daily lives. They found new confidence and developed consciousness of the social, economic, and political realities in their lives. They learned to analyze issues and work together as a community. They expressed their cultural identity through music, storytelling, and drama. Many acquired knowledge in home economics, parenting, nutrition, agriculture, and preventive health, giving them incentive and a very solid foundation for future learning.

Leaders of this program, however, recognize the need to improve. They are attempting to revise their culturally relevant reading primers, which are based upon learner-generated themes. These revisions are focused upon developing a linguistically sound sequence of fundamental reading skills. The revisions also include a problem-solving format that emphasizes critical thinking, cultural expression, and action. A good program is getting better.

Literacy and reading and writing fundamentals

Provo, Utah

Project Read's tutoring program achieves a respectable success rate in teaching fundamental reading and writing skills to adults. Skills are taught in a systematic, structured, sequential manner. Some higher-level reading and writing skills, including critical thinking, everyday writing, and reading for information and enjoyment, are part of the curriculum. Occasionally, students have opportunities for cultural appreciation and expression.

Common criticism: Learners are taught in isolation from their neighborhood and cultural context. As a result, very few of the marginalized poor—Spanish-speaking migrants and Native Americans—ever enroll for instruction, even though they represent a substantial portion of the nonreading population of the area. Passive learners are fed culturally irrelevant materials that teach the mechanics of reading, but don't really prepare learners to confront the causes of illiteracy or the greater educational and social issues that affect their lives.

Another view: Learners in this program have a goal—to master basic reading and writing skills. The program enables them to experience success in an instructional process that moves them toward this goal. The program's solid success rate demonstrates that students are achieving what they want to achieve. Enrollment is completely voluntary. Students gain fundamental reading and writing skills and some critical thinking skills which will provide a solid base for further learning in critical thinking, cultural expression, or any other content areas. Possessing fundamental reading skills is a good starting point for developing higher skills needed for full participation in society.

This program accomplishes what it sets out to achieve. Learners meet their goals. The program serves an extremely important and worthwhile purpose. However, if leaders hope to reach the underserved, marginalized poor of the community, they'll have to expand their program's horizons.

Literacy and the revolution

Nicaragua

In this national campaign, peasants throughout the Nicaraguan countryside learned certain basic reading skills, and had opportunities to develop critical thinking and cultural expression. Debate about the specific results of this campaign has become so politicized that it's hard to know the precise level of achievement. But the fact remains that a large number of participants who previously had no opportunities for formal education learned many literacy skills.

Common criticism: Because the primary goal of the Nicaraguan campaign was to increase support for the *Sandinista* regime, activities supposedly aimed at the development of critical thinking were really sessions in political indoctrination. Learners' passive acceptance of propaganda and lectures on Marxist ideology cannot be called critical thinking. The campaign was also incomplete in its teaching of fundamental listening, speaking, reading, and writing skills. And the program had no systematic follow-up reading materials to prevent people from losing their skills.

Another view: Every mass literacy campaign carries with it implicit ideological and cultural messages. There are no politically neutral literacy campaigns. But the Nicaraguan campaign was more overt than most in stating its political intent. According to accounts of the campaign, the participants were not coerced to participate. Voluntary participation and retention levels were fairly high, suggesting that learners had goals and enjoyed success in an instructional process that enabled them to meet those goals. It's unclear whether learners and instructors always shared the same goals. Such a discrepancy is a common problem in many literacy programs. And, admittedly, some of the campaign efforts did fit into the category of propaganda. But the dialogue and exchange that accompanied these presentations did encourage critical thinking. The evidence is clear that many, if not all, fundamental skills were taught. The campaign was effective in many ways.

Literacy and development

Philippines, near Cavite

This participatory community action effort doesn't call itself a literacy program. Its major purpose is not the teaching of fundamental skills. Yet its entire thrust is based upon learning. It effectively enables learners to develop many critical thinking skills and offers opportunities for cultural expression. It succeeds in fusing this learning with immediate action by the people to solve the problems they encounter daily.

Common criticism: This program failed in its attempt to incorporate fundamental reading and writing skills into its highly motivational learning and action projects. Development and community change projects often make the same tragic mistake of failing to incorporate the basics into the fabric of their learning and action programs. When their work is done, the people still lack the basic tools to gain access to information. They remain controlled by others.

Another view: This project's leaders recognize the importance of fundamental reading and writing skills, and they actively seek ways to incorporate reading and writing basics into the program. The program's success in developing fundamental listening and speaking skills, as well as including critical thinking, cultural expression, and action, should be acknowledged. In reality, this program offers its participants a fuller range of educational services than do many programs.

Literacy and social/political awareness

San Francisco

This urban project emphasizes critical thinking and some cultural expression. Many of the learners already have proficiency in some fundamental skills. Occasional tutoring helps those who seriously lack fundamentals. Action steps are sometimes discussed, but rarely implemented. Learners are challenged with dialogue and problem-solving exercises that develop their listening, speaking, reading, and writing skills to very high levels. This highly participatory learning process enables learners to critically examine the economic, racial, and social realities of their lives and to gain new attitudes, information, skills, and motivation to seek further learning.

Common criticism: This program doesn't deserve its title of "Project Literacy." It doesn't set out to teach fundamental reading skills. Despite all the rhetoric about raising consciousness and developing skills in reflection and analysis, the program leaves many of its participants with reading deficiencies that will prevent them from applying their critical thinking skills once they leave.

Another view: The program views itself as a literacy program because it helps learners increase their capacity for comprehension, critical analysis, and information gathering. The learners use written and spoken language to gain access to various information sources and reach independent conclusions about what they hear and read. Learners begin to make choices and decisions on the basis of information they select and analyze. They become more aware of the broader social, political, and economic realities that affect their individual and community experience. They begin to question and confront oppressive societal forces in their environment. They seek to identify the causes of, and alternative responses to, the problems in their daily lives.

The participants of the program represent cultural and racial minority populations. For the most part, they are poor and have had negative experiences with formal education. For many learners, their experience in this program reverses a lifelong sense of alienation and failure with educational experiences. Participants provide much of the leadership of the program and become deeply committed to its success.

As a natural by-product of this highly motivational learning experience, all participants improve their reading skills. The program doesn't claim to teach all the fundamental skills, but it does enable learners to experience success in a learning process that helps them meet their goals.

The unmet challenge

Millions of adults in the United States with insufficient literacy skills, and hundreds of millions worldwide, remain unserved. The challenge for programs that are currently successful is to reach more people in better ways. Programs and organizations wishing to reach those unserved or underserved socioeconomic groups with the greatest need should consider one or more of the following objectives:

Find ways to affirm and support each other. The five programs just discussed demonstrate that many kinds of literacy efforts can be effective. But they could be even more effective if they found ways to support each other. Such affirmation of the successes of those with different approaches opens the way for new networks of collaboration and expands the possibilities for greater impact.

Serve greater numbers of learners in existing ways. This objective requires programs to do what they already do well, but do more of it. This includes more staff, more volunteers, more training, and more students.

Improve the quality or range of instruction. This improvement could involve an increase in the number of learners served. Some improvements involve changed techniques, learning activities, or materials. Others involve increasing the range of what is taught. Programs focused on fundamental skills may seek to expand to include critical thinking and cultural expression. Programs focused on critical thinking may seek to include fundamental skills more systematically. Some programs that offer some critical thinking skills may want to offer even more in this area or in the areas of cultural expression and action.

Serve new learner audiences. Those who need literacy services the most tend to be the last to receive adequate opportunities to learn. Members of minority populations, people who reside in inner-city slums, or other groups who are disenfranchised and poor are typically least likely to enroll or succeed in standard literacy programs. The reasons for this failure rest less with the learners than with the organization and methodologies of the program. Successfully involving these so-called "hard-to-reach" learner populations requires some very nontraditional approaches. Programs that want to serve these groups will need to consider types of organization, instruction, and learner participation appropriate to the task.

Pursuing these objectives will move programs closer to the literacy-for-social-change model. It will not necessarily be easy, as it will involve conscious change. The following pages introduce several of the areas in which new attitudes, techniques, and approaches may be needed, along with some possible risks and trade-offs.

Part II
Plans and Assumptions

Chapter 4

How to get started

What steps does a group or community take to launch and sustain a learning program that successfully integrates the four components of literacy for social change?

There is no single infallible procedure to follow, no all-purpose formula that fits every community, cultural setting, and organizational structure. But there is a consistent pattern with common elements that can serve as a model. Literacy-for-social-change programs result from conscious, deliberate efforts and planning.

Key decisions

Leaders of any literacy program must make decisions that ultimately shape its nature and design. Robert F. Caswell has described six key elements of literacy programs subject to such decision making. They are:

Philosophy/goals. What are the learning program's overall purpose and goals? How does the program define literacy? What constitutes success?

Learners. Who are they? Where do they live? What communities or neighborhoods participate in the learning program?

Instructors. Who are the teachers, facilitators, and/or leaders of the learning process? How are these instructors chosen? Who plans and/or implements the educational experience?

Methods/materials. What methods are used to facilitate learning? What is the content of learning, and what materials are used in this process? In what setting and location does learning take place?

Funding. Where do financial and other resources come from? To what extent do funding sources shape the program?

Administration and decision making. Who makes major decisions and how are these decisions made? Some argue that decision making is the single most important element of a literacy program design, because decision makers can determine all the other elements of the program. A conflict between the interests of learners and the priorities of the decision-making structure would probably be resolved in favor of those with the power to decide.

Programs that work successfully with the poor and disenfranchised are likely to emphasize leadership, instructors, methods, and materials that are consistent with the perspective of the learner. In other words, learning usually occurs near where the learners live, and learners play a strong, active role in leadership and instruction.

In the evolution of any literacy program, though, specific characteristics of these decision areas will change over time. For example, a change in board membership, staffing, or the learners can generate shifting priorities regarding goals, students, instructors, or materials. Leaders should remain sensitive to the interrelation of these factors and attempt to make decisions based upon the overall impact of any given action.

Steps for initiating the process

Keeping in mind all of these key design elements, some specific steps are necessary to direct a process toward the literacy-for-social-change model. These steps may be taken in the traditional sequence listed below, they may follow a different sequence, or several steps may occur simultaneously. The steps are as follows:

1. Site survey
2. Program entry points
3. Thematic research and initial materials development
4. Initial organization for learning
5. Learning method and content
6. Linking learning and action
7. Evaluation and revision
8. Planning for autonomous program development

Site survey. This step is an information-gathering process that leads to a decision. At one extreme, it may be informal, intuitive, and general; at the other, highly formalized and comprehensive.

A site survey may be as simple as an afternoon visit to a given neighborhood or as elaborate as a two-year, in-depth study. But in practice, it's likely to fall somewhere between these extremes.

Minimally, a site survey gathers demographic information about the prospective learning community, including some sense of popular issues, needs, and interests. It should also identify possible program entry points, including natural leaders, potential partner groups, and community concerns that may generate learner involvement. Site surveys may also project possible learning objectives, prospective learning sites and materials, and a whole range of information related to each of the six key elements of program design.

How extensive does a site survey need to be? It should provide at least enough information for leaders to make a basic yes-or-no decision ("Do we expend the energy and resources to start a literacy program or at least actively test the possibilities?").

Program entry points. The site survey may or may not identify prospective program entry points. A program entry point is simply a place to begin. Generally, it involves locating leaders or agencies who represent issues and opportunities of great interest to potential learners. A fine entry point would be the widespread desire of people to learn to read and write along with neighborhood or village leaders anxious to see a learning program get started. Often, though, the entry point is connected to some area of community interest other than reading and writing.

Leaders need to decide whether they want to start with an action project or a learning agenda. Should they initiate a community action project that will generate a learning process, and ultimately add a basic reading and writing component to the learning agenda? Or do they want to begin with reading and writing fundamentals that will lead to an action project? Many times, these two entry points can be combined.

In 1988, for example, Guillermina (Guille) López Bravo, director of Laubach work in central Mexico, was exploring the development of a literacy program in a cluster of nine isolated *ranchos* north of the city of Irapuato. She considered three possible entry points, none of which directly incorporated basic reading and writing instruction. She visited informally with villagers and found many who were interested in learning to play the guitar. Guille could teach it, but she realized from past experience that guitar instruction would be so consuming of time and energy that she rejected the idea.

Another possible entry point was the obvious concern among villagers about the lack of health care. Guille's work with similar literacy projects in the vicinity gave her a familiarity with combining basic education and health care development. Guille discovered that the Guanajuato state school of nursing had expressed interest in training health workers in isolated rural areas. She realized that the school's training program could be a part of an overall literacy program and offered to assist in the recruitment and training of health workers from the *ranchos*. The school agreed, and with new resources and villagers who were interested in improving their health care, Guille began the recruitment effort. She began to explain how fundamental skills, cultural expression, and action projects were necessary to make the health care program successful and increase community productivity. Plans for basic reading instruction were discussed, and the seeds for establishing a literacy-for-social-change program were in place.

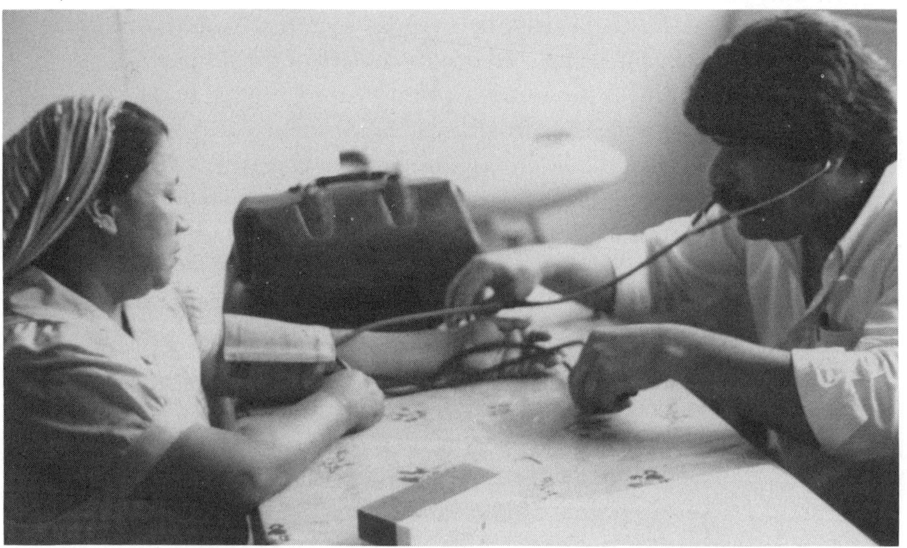

Health care needs provide a common entry point for many isolated, rural communities wishing to launch a literacy-for-social-change program.

While working on the health issue, Guille found another entry point. Some of the local leaders became interested in opportunities for women to increase their meager income through sewing projects. The women were introduced to others who had succeeded in forming a successful women's sewing cooperative as part of a literacy initiative. The idea caught hold and the women began simple sewing projects which Guille helped them sell to the Guanajuato hospital. These action steps in health and income generation would soon be integrated in a total literacy learning process.

Thematic research and initial materials development. Seven men wearing the traditional peasant *dhoti* skirt of rural Bangladesh sat on the ground at the edge of a rice paddy. Speaking Bengali, the men engaged in animated conversation. They discussed their experiences in the marketplace and spoke of feeling confused or cheated in transactions involving measurement or counting. One of the group recorded the discussion on tape and jotted down field notes as he continued to ask questions. Another participant sketched a simple line drawing of the scene that the men described. Thematic research and materials development for a literacy project were under way.

The local artist and recorder were attempting to document the reality of the prospective learners' lives. They conducted several individual and group interviews with peasants to identify issues and experiences that the people felt were important and basic in their lives. Those interviewed spoke informally about many daily-life concerns related to housing, health, nutrition, transportation, the marketplace, and other topics. They also described positive aspects of their culture and community.

Later, the recorder returned and asked questions that expanded upon the earlier discussions. The artist showed his sketches to participants, and they responded, "Yes, that's what happens," or in some cases, "No, it isn't like that." Sketches and notes were revised to convey a more accurate account of the participants' perspective of reality.

From the interviews and sketches, a number of phrases, words, and topics repeatedly emerged that suggested learning and action themes of intense interest to these learners.

A committee of village participants had been organized to join the interviewer and artist to discuss the prospective themes. One such theme appeared to be related to marketplace concerns. Notes from the marketplace discussion yielded such frequently repeated words as *money, market, pay, price,* and *buy.* Committee members reviewed the notes and discussed the topic. They felt that one oft-repeated word from the interviews, *cheat,* best reflected the essence of the villagers' concern. They selected this word not only because it powerfully expressed the feelings of the people, but because in their language, it is a simple word that lends itself to the limited reading vocabulary of a new reader.

The committee considered many key words and themes. These words were compared and arranged to provide a key vocabulary list, introducing words in an order that enabled the learner to experience a sequential progression. For this reason, some difficult words were dropped from the list in favor of simpler words that still conveyed strong meaning. The primer that finally emerged included a marketplace sketch that provoked energetic dialogue.

All thematic research efforts needn't be identical to the Bangladesh experience. They should reflect the existing literacy proficiency as well as the concerns of the learner group. Instead of sketches, photography may be used. Sometimes photographs or sketches are gathered after the words have been selected. Frequently, thematic research yields simple stories that can be used to reinforce reading lessons. Songs, skits, crafts, dance, poetry, history, or community action project ideas may also emerge from the thematic research process. On the other hand, where resources are extremely sparse, even sketches or photographs may not be possible.

Regardless of the mechanics, effective thematic research yields themes, vocabulary, and other documentation that genuinely mirror the aspirations of those who will go through the instructional process.

Initial organization for learning—the "big meeting." The essence of this initial organization step is the generation of commitment and a sense of ownership in the upcoming educational process. This is far more likely to happen if learners experience a process that enables them to articulate their reasons for learning. Prospective participants need to discover that their ideas and concerns matter and that the learning program will help them to address these concerns.

As a natural part of the site survey, program entry, and thematic research processes, many community leaders and prospective learners may have already become interested and involved in the program. Committees for materials development and other projects may have been organized. The more active the participation of prospective learners in these earlier steps, the greater the prospects for successful recruitment in the actual learning program.

Through the interviews and informal conversations of the site survey and thematic research, many individuals may have already decided to join, but overall success requires a group commitment as well. Without a community consensus to participate, real community change will never happen. Individual and group commitment generally occurs at one or a series of "big meetings." The big meeting is a public gathering that allows prospective learners and concerned community participants to discuss the issues raised through thematic research, to consider the possible benefits of educational efforts related to these issues, and to express their desire to participate.

Participants assemble for a big meeting in a remote community in Nepal.

The big meeting can involve a limited, targeted group such as the prospective members of one class, or a large, general audience such as anybody in a given village or neighborhood who is interested in finding out more. Often, a series of initial meetings is required to allow people to test the possibilities before making a final commitment. The meeting itself may be structured with motivational testimonials by local leaders about community issues as well as the benefits of the learning program, and demonstrations of the prospective learning materials. The meetings may also be highly informal and based solely upon group discussion. To achieve genuine commitment, however, participants must have opportunities to express their feelings and to connect their aspirations with the goals of the program. These meetings may even shape the curriculum of the educational program.

With group consensus to support the learning effort, important organizational decisions can be made at or following the meeting. Scheduling and grouping of classes can take place.

Some suggest that the number of learners in a basic literacy group not exceed fifteen. Others aim for twenty to twenty-five. In many cases, reading skill levels among interested participants will vary drastically. Frequently, learning groups are organized according to basic literacy, secondary literacy, postliteracy discussion groups, and other courses. *Campesinos* in Carmen, Colombia, formed a basic literacy class that met on Tuesday evenings, and a postliteracy discussion circle open to advanced and beginning readers that convened on Thursdays. Participants in the Lutheran Settlement House Women's Program in Philadelphia meet in groups ranging from beginning reading to high school equivalency. Individual participation in any given learning group may be based on testing, grade completion, neighborhood groupings, self-selection, or other criteria that make the most sense for that program.

Learning method and content. To be consistent with the literacy-for-social-change model, the content and method of instruction should be designed to integrate all four of its components. In many learning sessions each component can complement the others to create a whole far more powerful than the mere collection of separate exercises. Listening, speaking, reading, writing, and computation skills arise from the practical context of the learners' total cultural, social, and political environment. In this way, the aspirations of learners and the program can coincide.

But practice can fall short of the ideal. The conscious integration of all four areas is an ideal that in some sessions is flawlessly achieved and at other times fails to occur. The attempt can end up forced and abrupt. In any given session, the facilitator's limited skills, outside disruptions, or simply a "bad day" can foil the best of intentions. In some cases, learner interest in a given subject may suggest that, for a period of time, instruction should focus on just one of these learning goals. But such a focus is temporary, and over time an integrated balance is pursued. The cumulative result of successfully integrating these areas is a solid reward of motivation, retention, and action for change.

The development of instructional methods and materials that achieve this ideal is the result of conscious decision making. To what degree and in what ways should learners be involved in the decisions that shape the content of learning in the literacy-for-social-change model? One view suggests that although learners should state their learning goals, instruction should focus on prescribed skills and information needed to attain those goals. According to this view, motivation continues to grow as learners experience success and gain confidence. This process tends to be "teacher-guided." Another viewpoint suggests that the content of learning should be "learner-guided," and that a flexible curriculum should evolve with maximum learner direction. Both concepts have validity, and effective programs frequently practice a mix of these ideas.

Another important instructional issue deals with the scope of learning. Dr. Luís Oscar Londoño, director of Laubach South American programs, suggests that two intersecting continuums of instructional focus should be remembered. One range deals with time, starting with the past, moving to the present, and then to the future. The other deals with perspective—beginning with the individual and leading out to the family, the neighborhood, the broader local community, the region, the state, the nation, and the world. Generally, learning is most effective if the focus begins in the past and present and at the individual, family, and local levels. Beginning learners identify most readily with concrete local realities of yesterday and today. Gradually, the focus of discussion and analysis can shift to the regional, state, national, and international dimensions of issues with a look toward the implications for the future.

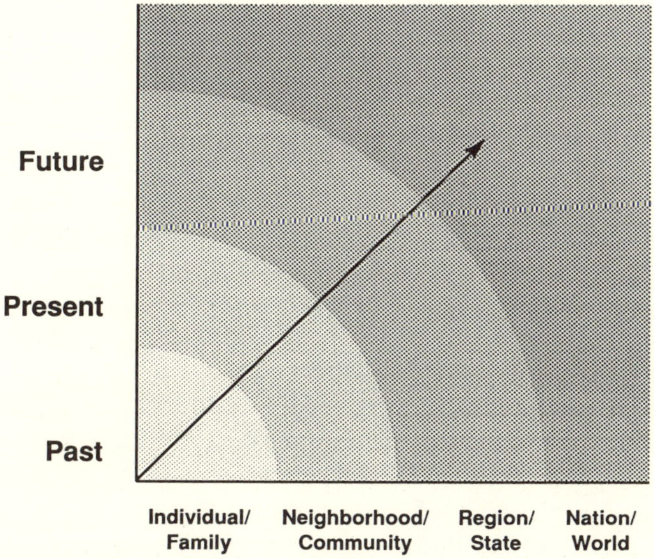

Future
Present
Past

Individual/ Family
Neighborhood/ Community
Region/ State
Nation/ World

A successful literacy learning process tends to begin at the center of the axis and move outward.

Linking learning and action. To ensure that the literacy effort moves beyond mere problem posing to problem solving, program leaders must consciously seek opportunities for group action. Sometimes, these action projects flow naturally from the discussion of learner-generated themes. For example, learners in Tabasará, Panama, discussed the poor nutrition of their children and jointly decided to plant a communal garden and to learn how to grow more nutritious foods.

Often, meaningful projects require logistical support that in turn requires some very active leadership. Literacy learners in the Laubach program in Tinaja de Negrete, Mexico, had a very strong interest in health issues. An aggressive program leader began exploring available resources and found state health officials willing to share medical supplies and training for first aid. They were also willing to help establish *botequines* (medicine chests) in each *rancho*. The health action focus has gradually broadened as village health committees have led the way to a number of initiatives, including the building and staffing of a village clinic. Without outside resources, the options for group action related to health would have been severely limited. As much as possible, learners should provide the leadership in obtaining these resources and planning the project. As a practical matter, though, program leaders may have to take initiative to ensure that action does occur.

Action projects that enable learners to experience confidence and success in addressing problems are a logistical challenge. They require lots of work and follow-up and invariably overlap with the work of other agencies concerned with such issues as health, transportation, agriculture, and housing. Such agencies may become partners or resources in the process. A successful educational effort must be committed to crossing traditional boundaries of practice. The most profound educational outcomes have been realized as people act upon their life concerns. That means that educators are in the community development business and community developers need to be educators.

Genuine community change and development are the result of new attitudes, information, and skills among the people. Outside initiatives to build wells, improve housing, or increase livelihood are of limited and temporary value if the people aren't empowered with the confidence and capacity to "own," maintain, and build upon these projects. A literacy effort can even begin with an action project, as long as the learning agenda is clearly in mind at the outset. Education becomes the primary activity, and as people develop new abilities and perspectives through the successful implementation of an action project, they are prepared to master new and ever more complex skills and information.

Action projects are absolutely vital to the success of the educational effort. They can often be initiated in response to particular resource opportunities, such as a housing mini-grant, or a willing buyer for homemade items, or training funds for village health workers. Someone must have the responsibility and authority to follow up on such opportunities. These opportunities may even become the program entry points for a successful literacy-for-social-change program. Resource opportunities are important, but real change demands that action projects be consistent with the expressed needs of the people and based upon a consciously developed educational curriculum.

Evaluation and revision. Literacy-for-social-change efforts are often experimental. A program grows out of the unique needs and interests of a given community of learners. Each program site has specific cultural, historical, geographic, and economic conditions that help shape it. Programs successful in generating community change are by nature dynamic and growing. These realities underscore the need for ongoing evaluation and revision to keep the program effective and in touch with the aspirations and needs of learners. As learners gain greater capacity, the roles of leaders, instructors, funders, and especially the learners will change. A program design that may have been effective in the early stages of program development may not be appropriate later on. The challenge for effective leaders is not to resist change, but to use it to maximum advantage.

Planning for autonomous program development. The ultimate test of the effectiveness of a literacy-for-social-change program comes after any funders or leaders who are not members of the learning community have left. The process of learning that makes possible community change and development should be perpetual. The goal of all the research, materials, classes, and action projects is to develop a lasting base of skills, information, and attitudes to unite the community and solve problems on an ongoing basis. To develop such a foundation takes time. Program funders and leaders should develop a program of learning and action that lasts anywhere from three to ten years with autonomous local leadership in full control at the end. In fact, at every step of the process, learners should prepare for independent leadership by taking the lead whenever possible in planning, instruction, action, and evaluation. When every phase of the program truly belongs to the people, the literacy-for-social-change ideal has been achieved.

The following chapters examine the many additional facets of the literacy-for-social-change model, ranging from general attitudes to nitty-gritty techniques. Included are topics such as specific methods for integrating fundamental skills, critical thinking, cultural expression, action projects, and the development of a learner-guided and bicultural approach. Issues such as program decision making, the role of teachers as co-learners, materials development, and the potentially risky, political nature of the literacy-for-social-change model are also addressed.

These topics are interrelated. Sometimes to clarify a concept, a topic is presented as though it exists in isolation. It really doesn't. The full power of these approaches comes about when they form an integrated whole. Readers of these chapters may make a very wise and practical decision to select one or two aspects of the model to incorporate into their existing efforts. In so doing, practitioners should view their programs in a holistic and systematic way. Seemingly isolated changes in philosophy, method, materials, or administration can have a far-reaching impact. Needed changes should be embraced enthusiastically and made as quickly as possible while keeping in mind the broader potential consequences.

Chapter 5

Start with the learners.

In San Francisco, in 1983, some of the learners in Project Literacy developed a skit that expressed their feelings about formal schooling. In subsequent years, other groups have adapted this skit to fit the realities of their particular communities. The following adaptation was developed by a learning group located at the Dunbar Center in Syracuse, New York, in an inner-city black community.

The skit is short, simple, and provocative. Props include three chairs, a trash can, label cards (pieces of paper with words written on them big enough for the audience to see), and masking tape. Parts are played by three "actors" (anyone willing to perform). One plays the teacher, the two others play students.

The chairs are arranged in a row facing the audience. The teacher wears a label saying "teacher" and stands facing the audience. To the left of the teacher, seated on a chair, is the first student wearing a label that says "student." On the next chair, also wearing a label saying "student," is the second student. Seated on the third chair is the trash can which is also labeled "student."

The Bossy Teacher

Teacher: *(pompously, displaying label)* I am a teacher. I am an expert. I have authority. *(speaking to other cast members)* You are my students. I know what you need to learn. And I'm going to make sure you get the correct education. You must work hard and not be lazy. At this school, we have high standards and rules to follow. I expect you to remember the things I tell you.

Today's lesson is on American history. We're going to learn about how the slaves were freed. On this paper I'm handing out I have all the information I expect you to learn today. Study it carefully. In a moment we will have a test to see if you've learned what I expect, and to determine whether you are a good student or not.

(Students sit with hands held out. Teacher gives a sheet of paper to the First and Second Students and puts a third sheet in the trash can.)

Read it carefully. I expect you to give me back the information I've given you. *(Students study intently.)* OK, that's enough time. Now, I'll test you. Ms. (or Mr.) ______, this is a multiple choice quiz. Here's the question: Who freed the slaves, A) George Washington, or B) Abraham Lincoln?

First Student: Well, it seems to me that a lot of people freed the slaves. John Brown or Harriet Tubman. You could even say Martin Luther King freed people from slavery.

Teacher: Wrong! That's not the information I gave you. *(Teacher places label that says "flunked" on the forehead of the First Student.)* You flunked. You're not a good student. Now, our next student. Tell me Mr. (or Ms.) ______, who freed the slaves, A) George Washington, or B) Abraham Lincoln?

Second Student: *(nervous, intimidated)* I . . . uh.

Teacher: Look at your paper, dummy. The answer's right there. Just give me back the information I gave you.

Second Student: Uh, I don't read too good, but I do know something about slavery. Sometimes I think my landlord has me in slavery, and I . . .

Teacher: Wrong! You flunked. *(Places "flunked" label on student's forehead.)* You are not a good student. You students are obviously not motivated to get an education. *(Moves to trash can.)* Now, let's see how you do. Can you give me back the information I asked for? *(Lifts paper out of the trash can.)* Very good. You gave it back to me just the way I gave it to you. This is outstanding. *(Places A+ label on trash can.)* You are a very good student. You're the best.

The skit can be used with any group. Immediately following the performances, the facilitator should ask the audience questions to stimulate reflection. Some possible questions include:

- What happened in this skit?
- Why didn't the two students answer the questions the way the teacher wanted? Are they really "bad" students?
- To be "good" learners, do we have to be trash cans?
- Are the answers in a book or the ones a teacher gives necessarily the only or even the best answers? Can learners come up with good ideas that are different from the teacher's ideas?
- Are teachers always right?
- Should teachers be concerned with getting the "right" answer from students or helping people learn? Why?
- What do you want to learn?
- Can you learn without a teacher?
- How can we help each other learn?

The "bossy teacher" skit exemplifies one end of the spectrum of approaches to education, one in which the teacher and school play a controlling, dominant role. Most people who have been in school are familiar with this concept. As John Dewey, a pioneer of modern adult education, once noted, "Most teachers are too busy answering questions that students never ask."

Students often listen passively to a "bossy teacher," and then ignore or forget what they have been taught.

Courtesy The Hesperian Foundation

Stated in the extreme, this approach says the teacher and the educational institution know all the student needs to learn. Their role is to dispense prescribed knowledge. The skills and information to be taught are decided and packaged by the school or teacher and given to the student. Instruction may or may not be boring or irrelevant, but by definition it is controlled and directed by the instructor and the school. For most students and teachers this traditional emphasis is not a foreign idea. It is a prevailing norm within most educational programs, from elementary schools through universities.

Various groups who view this skit react in very different ways. Many identify with the students and express frustration with an educational system that from their experience has rewarded "right" answers and suppressed the learners' life perspective. A group of learners at the Dunbar Center offered some very unexpected responses, however. One woman commented that what the students in the skit said was a "mess of junk, not worth nothin'." One of the men noted that the students' answers were "wrong 'cause that's not what the teacher wanted." He continued, "School is important. It's rehearsal for life. You don't go anywhere in life without school."

It seemed as though these learners really felt the bossy teacher was right on target, and the students actually were "bad." These were surprising reactions from individuals who had dropped out of school and had avoided formal education all their lives. However, in response to the question, "Wasn't there anything the students said that was worthwhile?" the whole discussion shifted. A woman bravely shared her feelings. "Harriet Tubman was my great aunt. I think that's important." Suddenly, it was all right to say what was on their minds. Another blurted out, "Those students were smarter than the teacher. The teacher missed the whole point."

"That teacher was an educated fool," someone else declared. An educated fool "gots a diploma but can't do nothin' but strut around and brag on how smart they are." With blunt honesty, they talked about teachers, social workers, and policemen who they felt used their formal education to make things hard for "good" people, like themselves. From the learners' perspectives, school credentials represented oppression and arrogance. In the skit, the learners felt that the students' answers were important and valid. But they also knew that to the teacher, the "right" answer was the only answer.

They, like many learners, had experienced the difficulty of giving someone in control the "right" answer, an answer that is not necessarily the most important or self-affirming one. Their relationships with landlords, teachers, welfare workers, administrators, police, and others they described as "educated fools" had taught them some dehumanizing lessons. They had learned that it's important to say the "right" thing, even if it is humiliating, in order to get by in a world dominated by those who think of some people as "dumb trash." Although the atmosphere in the Dunbar learning circle was open, the participants initially felt that they had to say what the educated facilitator wanted to hear, and not what they really felt.

Students like these are stereotypically labeled as "apathetic," "unmotivated," and "tough to teach." Low educational test scores in the slums, ghettos, and reservations of the world perpetuate the notion. If educators wish to reach these "hard-to-serve" populations, they need to take a hard look at why such students are "apathetic" and "unmotivated." The answer, as many groups and organizations have found, often lies in their own approach to education, parodied here as the "bossy teacher." Instruction that is excessively teacher-guided will not reach the "hard to serve." In contrast, literacy for social change tends to emphasize a different approach, one that starts and ends with the people served. This approach can be characterized above all as learner-guided.

The learner-guided approach

"Learner-guided" may sound very much like a popular term in current use—"learner-centered" education. Learner-centered practices range from an occasional participatory classroom activity to a professed view that learners are the main concern of a program. Indeed, many very different programs describe themselves as learner-centered. Most probably include a significant portion of teacher-guided instruction.

The point is not to quibble over terminology, but to suggest that the true learner-centered program is the one that has balanced learner-guided and teacher-guided instruction, so that learners are able to meet their own learning goals.

Finding that balance is a challenge, especially because learner-guided approaches are not fully appreciated, practiced, or understood. And most educational efforts tend to favor a teacher-guided focus. Practitioners who are successful among poorer and disenfranchised learners, however, have found that effective education and development efforts require a greater understanding and application of learner-guided principles.

Learner-guided approaches respect the experiences and insights of the learners.
Courtesy The Hesperian Foundation

By definition, learner-guided instruction challenges stereotypes. It assumes that learners have abundant potential to learn and share—in spite of the injustices they must endure. Learner-guided practice emphasizes leadership, curriculum, and instruction that arise from the learners and the learners' lives. The instructors are viewed as co-learners and facilitators.

Learner-guided approaches build the educational experience around the life needs and goals of learners. Learners can increase their sense of self-worth when instruction is based on the experiences, insights, and issues of their lives. It's an inspiring prospect, but difficult to implement fully. Being a learner-guided facilitator demands humility and vulnerability in order to transcend the "bossy teacher" in all of us. Learner-guided sessions can be electric. They can also be terrifying. For many people, being a "bossy teacher" is easier and less threatening than being a learner-guided facilitator. And even the most effective, dedicated facilitators will make a number of practical trade-offs.

But with all the trade-offs, struggles, and contradictions, learner-guided approaches work. They can help empower the most oppressed and disenfranchised people to realize desperately needed social change. They can enable people to transcend barriers of race, religion, and class and achieve true solidarity. The learner-guided approach can provide the driving motivation needed to learn to listen, speak, read, write, compute, and think.

Does this mean the facilitator can't introduce important ideas and information or plan curriculum? Does it mean that teachers can't teach? Of course not. But it is important to remember the focal point. *Start with the learners.* Teachers ought not make the arrogant assumption that they know what students need and want to learn. Hardest of all, perhaps, is letting go of the desire to control. That means trusting—trusting students and oneself. Teachers must be co-explorers with students, helping them pose the questions that are important to them. In short, *you must learn from learners before you can really teach.*

How *does* one learn from learners? By actively listening to them, and by respecting them. This presupposes that there are very important things to discover from their lives and culture. This discovery occurs in two phases: 1) before the learners meet, and 2) when—and every time—the learners meet.

Before the learners meet

Ideally, learning from and about the participants begins long before they gather. When approached systematically, particularly as part of the development of instructional materials, this process is often referred to as "thematic research" (see chapter 4). However formal or informal, such a process should take place where the learners live—in their homes or neighborhoods. This way the facilitator can develop trust and rapport while discovering some of the objective conditions of the learners' lives and how they feel about those conditions.

A variety of formal tools to document the reality of the participants' lives may be needed, including field notes, tape-recorded conversations, photographs, and drawings. It may be a good idea to use demographic or historic research about conditions in the village or neighborhood.

When the learners meet

The learning session itself is the best forum for getting to know the learners. For example, when the Dunbar Center group discovered that their ideas counted, they were able to shape the direction and content of their learning.

This group was once described by the center's director as "dead end"—poor, unemployed, undereducated, alone, and unhealthy. Their learning sessions brimmed with gritty anecdotes. Janice, an older black woman, eagerly described her home brew for pest control. "I kill rats with peanut butter and Drāno. I make little balls of it and put it on the floor. By morning, they're dead."

Enthusiastically, others in the group shared their own formulas for dealing with cockroaches, violent drunks, and assorted illnesses. The learning sessions were filled with home remedies and tasty recipes. "A drop of turpentine in a spoonful of sugar saved my babies from the killing croup," declared one learner. They also shared secrets for repairing saddles, planting turnips, and double-stitching pants.

Politics and history were also discussed. One learner summed up the group's frustration in dealing with inconsistent and dehumanizing public welfare practices. "It's a confusing time down at the County Building," she said. Lively discussions developed on neighborhood issues, local government, community geography, family history, music, and culture. The group shared several learning goals, although they weren't always explicitly stated.

One tangible measure of a given activity's success is how much the facilitator has learned. Facilitators won't learn unless learners express themselves. A lecture or film by itself won't allow the facilitator to learn anything from the participants. Dialogue and other forms of expression should allow, or rather encourage, participants to voice their viewpoints and struggle with issues and concerns. At times, in accordance with the goals of learners, facilitators will need to present structured information or content. But the synergy of shared perspectives creates a new and richer understanding that no facilitator alone could have conveyed.

As needed, facilitators provoke questions, stimulate response, provide information, and paraphrase or summarize. The dynamics of the process require them also to be astute listeners and observers. After a learning session, the facilitators should ask themselves, "What did I learn today with the participants?" If the answer is "a great deal," the session was probably highly successful for everyone.

The facilitator's art

The facilitator has two objectives: 1) to develop and maintain rapport and mutual trust, and 2) to understand the participants and ultimately enable them to express their reality and their goals for learning.

To achieve the second objective, the facilitator synthesizes diverse and disjointed fragments from the participants' lives into a meaningful whole, helping them extract the essence of seemingly rambling discussions. The facilitator also helps the group to establish shared goals for learning by asking questions that learners answer through dialogue. Dialogue typically begins with a photo, a story, a skit, a song, a poem, a history, or some other form of expression that reflects the learners' lives. Such reflections, if effective, will raise many questions for discussion and trigger the dialogue process.

Freire calls such pictures, stories, or events that reflect the learners' perspective and provoke dialogue a "codification," or "code" of the learners' reality. Others have expressed this concept as an "illustration," a "documentation," a "powerful learning," or a "creative trigger." Whatever term is used, it is a learning activity or document that stimulates participant expression. It is more than simply an attention-getting step. Its creation should be the result of learner-guided research. It motivates learner involvement because it reflects the essence of what people feel is important in their lives.

If a reading lesson is part of the session, then the "powerful learning" will probably also include a key vocabulary word that captures the spirit of the photo or story. Freire calls such a key word a "generative" word, generated from the reality of the participants' lives. Generative words and discussion frequently also include an examination of letter sounds and phonetic combinations that can be derived from the original key word. Participants can make the powerful emotional connection between written words and concerns that hold great personal meaning in their own lives.

Participants as facilitators

In the development of a codification or the selection of generative words, learners can play a creative or decision-making role. Frequently, committees of learners or former learners participate in the creation of learning activities, the selection of key vocabulary for discussion, and peer tutoring. They also lead discussions. Such participation enhances learning and frees a single person from the entire load. Not only should facilitators be co-learners, but learners can and should become co-facilitators. Part of the learning process should be the development and encouragement of leadership from among learners.

Pictures and stories that reflect learners' lives help participants such as these in Nepal express their reality and their goals for learning.

The facilitator's perspective

The facilitator is frequently a bridge between two cultural perspectives—that of the learners and that of the dominant outside society. And being a bridge can be perplexing, even painful. As one facilitator in New Jersey commented, "It can be confusing to have your head in two different places at the same time." Sometimes it hurts to be stretched across the gap of two cultural worlds. At the same time, such a dual perspective is a great source of fulfillment and reward. If the learning process is effective, the learners will also begin developing a similarly broader perspective.

From where should facilitators be recruited? From one perspective, the ideal facilitator would be one of the learners. This person would literally share the viewpoint of the learners. On the other hand, the facilitator needs some degree of education, training, and experience not typically found among the learner population. Facilitators will almost always experience a degree of conflict between these two perspectives. Typically, the more experienced and educated they become, the further their own life outlook becomes removed from that of the participants. It's one of the many contradictions that facilitators and other leaders must recognize and deal with.

In many ways, learner-guided education, with all its flexibility and shared control, defies traditional curriculum planning. Effective facilitators don't seek absolute control like the "bossy teacher" does. But they must ensure that the process has direction and continuing purpose. This is sound educational practice, and moreover, many external conditions may require it. Some funding sources will support a learner-guided program focus, but may demand that certain predetermined skills (such as reading and writing basics) be included and tested in the process.

Prepared facilitators come to a given session with a "bag of tools," which includes a number of alternative learner-inspired activities. The most relevant learning activities are those that emerge from your specific learner group; however, activities inspired by other groups can also be useful. Chapter 7 includes several examples of learning activities from various literacy projects to stimulate your own creative thinking and learning.

Centuries ago Plutarch observed, "Man [and woman] is not a vessel to be filled, but a fire to be kindled." Facilitators who master their craft are fire starters—and they help keep the flames burning.

Chapter 6

Who are the leaders?

To be successful, literacy projects need committed leadership, sound organization, and wise decision making. The same principle that assures successful learner-guided instruction applies. *Start with the learners.*

An educational program whose true success depends upon learner participation, learner ownership, and learner development needs to be organized around its reason for existence, the learners. Learner goals and needs form a necessary part of the leadership structure. Curriculum development and evaluation criteria should be influenced by those who are most directly affected by the program—the learners.

This principle may seem overwhelmingly obvious, but in practice, it is often ignored. When it comes to administration, those who should be first often end up last.

As literacy leaders struggle with planning, the most important decision-making resource, the learner, is typically left out of the structure and process. Sometimes, leaders are willing to entertain change when they consider the potential of learners as program decision makers. All too often, though, the entrenched attitude is one of paternalism. The program exists to help "undereducated illiterates" and to rid the community of a big problem. This approach may be adequate for programs that serve "the cream of the crop," those self-recruiting learners who voluntarily seek out basic reading and writing instruction. These highly motivated, deserving students learn rapidly, and the programs validly claim success.

But the majority of nonreading adults, in the United States and worldwide, those with the greatest need for learning, come from poorer and disenfranchised populations. They tend to represent a minority perspective very different from that of the leaders. The failure of literacy programs to serve such audiences is partly related to the fact that the perspective of such learners is not incorporated in the planning and decision-making hierarchy. The goals of prospective learners from marginalized communities are not part of the program. Common program challenges, such as the difficulty in learner recruitment, high drop-out rates, and poor learner attendance, can be symtomatic of management deficiency.

If learner goals and needs are not part of the leadership structure, how can the structure be changed? Organizational change is always threatening. Some new people, namely the learners, are going to gain some power that they didn't have before. The starting point for change is a leadership commitment to learner involvement, with a focus on identifying learner goals and finding an instructional process that meets those goals. This is true at all levels, from national to village or neighborhood. Many organizations and groups are finding and using leadership from the ranks of their learners, from national organizations and centralized literacy campaigns to grassroots, local groups.

U.S. voluntary literacy organizations

In recent years, national voluntary literacy organizations in the United States—Laubach Literacy Action and Literacy Volunteers of America—have increased learner involvement in management and, to a much lesser degree, in instruction. Responding to the success and encouragement of local affiliates in learner-leadership activities, these national organizations have developed a variety of mechanisms to promote learner input.

Laubach Literacy Action has featured substantial student participation at its national conferences since 1984, co-sponsored two national student congresses, supported a new readers advisory committee, published a student newsletter and other resources to help local affiliates increase learner participation, and consistently encouraged programs to maximize learner input.

Likewise, Literacy Volunteers of America has featured substantial learner participation at its national conferences, published *Student Involvement Guidelines,* sponsored numerous local

At the 1989 Adult Literacy Conference, adult new readers from across the United States gathered to address issues ranging from employment to voting rights and citizenship responsibility.

special projects emphasizing student participation, and encouraged local affiliates to involve learners as leaders in management and small-group instruction.

Another national organization, the Association for Community Based Education, fosters the development of literacy programs within community-based organizations that typically already have a commitment to a strong participant leadership role.

While current progress is most encouraging, there remains considerable opportunity and need for further participation of learners in decision making and instruction at the national level.

The Colombian campaign

A unique national literacy campaign in Colombia has combined the centralized resources of the national government with a commitment to local, learner-centered programming and decision making. Dr. Luís Oscar Londoño, director of Laubach Literacy International's Latin American region, accepted a temporary assignment to direct planning for the campaign. In the spring of 1990, the campaign had entered the initial stage of implementation.

Wherever possible, the Colombian campaign identifies, works with, and strengthens existing grassroots organizations. Some of these groups already have extensive experience in literacy work and have developed thematic materials that reflect their individual perspectives. Groups of coal miners, coffee workers, urban slum dwellers, and sugar cane workers have each developed small networks and materials for literacy-for-social-change efforts among their constituencies. The campaign also adapts the groups' experiences and materials so they can be used to serve larger numbers of similar interest groups throughout Colombia. Other grassroots groups, such as unions, *campesino* cooperatives, women's groups, fishermen, and even some militant groups who have been opposed to the government in the past, are receiving aid as they develop their own basic and postliteracy learning materials.

This is a mass campaign, but programmatic decision making and practice, to the greatest extent possible, is decentralized and in the hands of learner constituencies. Rather than emphasizing a single set of uniform materials and methods, an array of learner-guided approaches is being applied. This pluralistic approach will undoubtedly generate some learning efforts with themes in opposition to current governmental policies and practices. Campaign leaders are willing to accept this diversity of perspectives.

Grassroots starting point

When the village committee in Tinaja was planning Tinaja's literacy program, they chose a learning approach that mostly celebrated village life and culture. They agreed to include some limited references to poor pay and sickness in the literacy materials, but they had no desire to dwell on the difficulties of life in the Tinaja region. They chose instead key words like *familia* and *fiesta*.

The Laubach consultant, Dr. Londoño, was frustrated with the committee's decision, but he recognized two realities. The committee members had been selected by the people, and his commitment to a learner decision-making process required him to respect their wishes, even if he didn't agree. He also realized that they might be correct in their assessment. They had all participated in a thematic research process with the prospective learners, and both serious issues and celebration themes had emerged. If the decision had been his alone, he would have emphasized the issues of land ownership, credit, poor health care, and lack of transportation that plagued the people. Yet he had to acknowledge that the representative committee knew the people far more intimately than he. Perhaps their approach would be more meaningful and motivational for the participants.

The committee prevailed, and time and the events that followed proved that their perspective was accurate. As it turned out, the emphasis on community celebration and unity was very well received. This approach set a climate for united community action. The low-key introduction of issues combined with this feeling of unity enabled the participants to learn and inspired joint action. Within a few years, the people had taken several concrete steps to address all of the issues that the consultant had wanted to emphasize.

Organizing for learner leadership

An outside agency can organize a grassroots literacy program from "scratch," but the effort is very difficult. The outside agency has the formidable task of winning the trust of neighborhood participants. A far simpler job is for an existing grassroots group to organize its own learner-guided literacy program. Outside agencies who may have some funds can invest in existing groups rather than attempt the more costly and generally less efficient step of starting their own program. Such an investment already sets the stage for decision making that is closer to the learners' perspective.

Within any organization that seeks learner leadership, the best place to begin is where the learners live, in their neighborhood or village. Whenever possible, planning meetings and especially learning sessions should be conducted near the participants' homes.

Come prepared first to listen. Go to people's homes and hear what their ideas and concerns are. Whether this is done by one facilitator or a committee of thematic researchers for materials development, this listening step serves many vital purposes. It enables planners to gain insight and information about the learners' lives to include in materials or learning activities. It sets a tone that lets the people know that this program cares about their perspective and ideas. Listening to learners on their turf generates learner interest in the program and helps stimulate recruitment. Dialogue with learners at this point can help identify prospective leadership.

An existing grassroots program may already have a decision-making structure that reflects the culture of the learner population. While such a structure may be invaluable, it is also wise to attempt to involve the actual learners in decision making. This can start as early as the first "big meeting."

Nearly every grassroots literacy program begins with at least one and probably several public recruitment or organizational meetings, usually publicized as part of the initial listening stage, in which prospective participants are invited to learn about and give input regarding the proposed literacy program. In some cases, the public meeting is the place where learning priorities are democratically decided. Prospective participants are given a chance to decide if they want to participate and offer their commitment to the program. Some mutually agreed upon ground rules may be set. Representative committees may be elected who in turn may develop curriculum or establish ongoing follow-up, evaluation, or community action.

In many communities where only some of the participants are in need of beginning reading skills and others have more advanced skills, groups may be divided according to beginning, intermediate, advanced, and postliteracy levels. Some projects, whose major purpose is to teach reading and writing basics, may still hold such meetings to organize learner committees. In some cases, more advanced readers are selected as team leaders or peer tutors to assist the facilitator in planning and instruction.

Based upon the consensus achieved at the "big meeting(s)," the actual learning sessions are scheduled and initiated. Each program follows the process in its own way.

Haiti's parish committees. A Haiti-wide literacy campaign sponsored by the Catholic church combined centralized resources with learner-guided methods and participant leadership. The campaign was not evangelical, and participation was not limited to church members. The uniform materials were based upon generative words and learner themes. Each geographic area of operation coincided with parish boundaries. Participant committees at the local parish level concerned themselves with facilitator training, program follow-up, evaluation, and postliteracy classes. The decentralized leadership structure worked very well, but participants complained that the national church leadership occasionally superseded local decision makers, and then things didn't run as effectively. The national church sponsorship of the campaign has been discontinued, but many local committees continue to function and provide excellent literacy programs.

Generative words and learner themes form the basis for French Creole literacy instruction in Haitian communities.

Learner decision making in the inner city. In the Syracuse, New York, Dunbar Center literacy project, the elderly black learners made curriculum decisions by majority vote. They had gathered three weeks earlier for their first "big meeting," responding to word-of-mouth invitations and handwritten flyers urging them to gather to talk about "things you feel are important." Free refreshments enhanced attendance the first time, but people came back with enthusiasm to develop a list of their priority concerns. In a sort of brainstorming format, participants generated nineteen key-word topics, including such themes as *welfare, rent,* and *jobs*. People spoke passionately about the value of their particular theme, and then they voted. The theme with the most votes was *food stamps*. It was discussed first in three subsequent sessions. The theme with the next number of votes was discussed second, the next treated third, and so on.

Each theme became the basis of lessons in reading and writing as well as dialogue, experience sharing, and group action. Facilitators helped organize the discussions and move the process forward, but generally the direction was dictated by the combined will of the participants.

Native leadership, North Kenya. Trained facilitators from the village conducted the literacy sessions in the Gabbra language. All the people were learning together, but whenever dialogue raised issues that might involve a community decision, the facilitators deferred leadership to the tribal decision-making structure. The village elders, although less formally educated than the facilitators, conducted discussions that would result in a united village action. In this way, literacy dialogue and community action became combined.

Grassroots money management, Southern California. José, Dolores, and all the other *barrio* committee leaders had discussed the $5,000 grant during several sessions. The funds were for the neighborhood literacy program, but otherwise had few requirements attached. Deciding the best way to spend the money became quite involved. Most of the learners got into the discussion. An outside observer might have suggested that all this participation in a simple fiscal decision could have been handled much more "efficiently." But during the previous eight years, the program had never had any money. Decisions made by one or two leaders could have caused dissension in the highly participatory neighborhood group. A sense of broadly shared ownership inspired tremendous ongoing voluntary support by a broad range of participants. Making quick judgements about the money might have saved time, but it would have undermined the powerful community support that was worth far more than a few thousand dollars.

The creative challenge

The patterns and possibilities for learner involvement in management and instructional decision making are myriad. The potential payoff is also tremendous. Those who recognize this potential have the creative opportunity to influence the development of such participation within their own spheres of concern. Through writing, research, planning, or practice, advocates of learner participation can encourage specific experiments or activities that initiate or increase participant leadership. The aim is to assure that learner needs and goals are expressed in management and curriculum decisions and that the instructional process is successful in addressing those goals.

Part III

The Four Components: A Closer Look

Chapter 7

Fundamental skills: foundation for change

In 1989, leaders from literacy-for-social-change programs in Bolivia, Mexico, and Colombia met in Cartagena, Colombia. For three days, they discussed the oppressive social and political realities that confront disenfranchised literacy learners. They described community action initiatives that respond to these realities, such as communal gardens and wells, village production and selling enterprises, and housing and road improvements. They spoke of *campesino* health initiatives, cooperative stores, and family credit programs. They reported on local cultural celebrations in music, dance, drama, and history. They spoke of community organization, indigenous leadership development, group problem solving, and local program autonomy. They discussed the transformation of communities in which people could now meet basic human needs and address the daily concerns of their lives.

All of the delegates represented literacy programs sponsored by Laubach Literacy International, yet in all their discussions about literacy education and action, there was no mention of basic reading and writing skills. One outside observer interrupted the discussion with questions that puzzled the group: "Is it possible to achieve the kind of just society your programs seek if large numbers of its people lack basic listening, speaking, reading, writing, and math skills? Do these basic skills have a place in your literacy programs?"

The group, startled at first, had a unanimous response. The delegates articulated what they thought was an unstated, but obvious, truth—*basic skills are fundamental to community change.* There can be no just society in which many members lack control of the language of their lives. They then stated explicitly that their programs emphasize classes in reading and writing fundamentals. While problem-posing discussion groups, cultural programs, and a host of community action projects flourish, there is always a basic skills component.

The distinguishing characteristic of a literacy-for-social-change program, moreover, is not just that it includes basic skills in a much broader "curriculum" for community change, but that all the components—basic skills, cultural expression, critical thinking, and action projects—are integrated. Each component is made relevant to and supportive of the other.

No recipe exists for the best way to teach basic skills. Much depends on the existing proficiencies of the learners and the literacy requirements of their local situation, as well as on their own goals.

Programs do, however, need to examine their assumptions regarding the nature of reading and writing as they design a curriculum. There is currently more than one school of thought regarding the definition of reading and how to teach it. A traditional approach holds that basic reading should be taught in a structured, sequential way. Simple preselected skills are taught as a foundation for increasingly difficult skills in a systematic sequence that ultimately includes all the fundamentals. Another approach starts from the premise that reading is a process less rooted in individual skills than in the contextual meaning of written communication. From this perspective, learning all the separate skills does not necessarily add up to comprehending total meaning.

This book doesn't propose a final answer to the question of how to teach reading. But the following pages examine issues for leaders to consider as they develop their own curriculum for teaching basic skills, along with examples of how some literacy-for-social-change programs have answered these same questions. This chapter concludes with a list of effective techniques and exercises used by practitioners in several countries to teach basic skills, and to initiate cultural expression and action projects.

Choosing and developing materials

Should literacy programs develop their own materials or purchase published items from the outside? This question is one practical starting point for approaching the issue of how to teach reading and writing in what sort of curriculum. To answer the question, some fictional colleagues of opposing persuasions —Professor Homegrown, Chairman Storebought, Mr. Remedial, Dr. Broadview, and Ms. Mix—will argue this question and suggest a broad range of underlying issues.

Professor Homegrown: I detest purchased literacy materials. They stifle participation and dialogue. It's impossible to conduct learner-guided literacy instruction with materials that are published outside the community of learners. These materials reflect generic themes with general application on a broad scale. If they can't deal with themes of immediate relevance to the learner population, then they're boring. They lack the power to motivate, and they don't generate dialogue and critical thinking.

In contrast, homegrown materials and learning activities developed with and by learners can address the specific issues and cultural themes of immediate interest to learners. Such materials allow for flexibility and tailored response to specific learner needs. They allow the programs and the learners to take responsibility and control of the learning process. There really is no other way.

Chairman Storebought: Professor Homegrown, you are unrealistic. Do you have any idea how time-consuming and expensive locally developed materials are? Many programs that center on learners opt for commercially developed materials because they don't have the experience, cash, or staff time to develop their own. Frankly, most attempts at locally developed materials are clumsy and amateurish.

Motivation is important, but teaching reading basics requires structured, sequential skills instruction. Learners need the progressive foundation of specific fundamental skills to master reading. Without sequential instruction, they gain bits and pieces of vocabulary and skills, but they won't attain integrated mastery of the written word. They need a comprehensive, systematic treatment of all the skills involved in reading. Preparing materials takes a trained linguist to assure that all skills are presented in proper order. That capacity is beyond the reach of local programs. If people who really want to learn to read are doing so in a technically efficient manner, their increasing success in acquiring skills will provide all the motivation needed to keep them learning. After they learn basic reading, they can get involved in community issues if they choose.

Mr. Remedial: This debate is silly. You've both missed the point. It doesn't matter where materials are developed as long as they're interesting. Some reading materials are motivational even if they don't have anything to do with the learners' specific cultural condition.

And frankly, this business of structured, sequential skills instruction is all out of proportion. Nearly every adult has some reading skills. That's why I say literacy programs are really remedial reading efforts. People need to get drawn into positive reading experiences from any source, homegrown or commercial, so they can get back into the routine of learning. The human brain can sort out a lot of those sequential skill problems if the participants are in a positive learning environment. Besides, the process of reading is more connected to finding meaning than to a collection of individual skills. Learners can fill in the gaps in vocabulary or grammar if they relate to the context of communication. Good literacy materials engage learners in fun and interesting experiences with the written word.

Dr. Broadview: You're all nit-picking. Yes, literacy involves basic reading skill instruction. That's what you're all talking about. Your points are very interesting, but they're irrelevant to the big picture. Literacy includes listening, speaking, writing, and math, not just reading, and it is experienced not just at the basic decoding level, but at levels involving critical thinking, cultural expression, and action projects. Moreover, literacy learning materials must reflect all of these goals. A comprehensive collection of literacy materials should be based upon the goals of learners. It should include basic skills primers as well as cultural materials, materials that stimulate dialogue through their treatment of critical individual and community issues, and guides that help in the implementation of action projects and community organization. Often, these materials can overlap in purpose. A basic reading primer can deal with cultural and community themes. But by all means let's not get bogged down in unnecessary detail about basic skills materials.

Ms. Mix: Dr. Broadview, your points are well taken, but the details you describe are hardly unnecessary. And Mr. Remedial, Professor Homegrown, and Chairman Storebought, there's more to this question than any one of you acknowledge. I'm glad I get the last word in this debate because you're all wrong, yet at the same time, you're all correct. Perhaps I can put your arguments in perspective. The question of literacy materials involves all of the factors you've talked about. But all of these factors have to be balanced in accordance with specific learner and program needs. Each program has to determine its own "right" mix of homegrown versus storebought materials. That mix should take all of your concepts into account.

For example, many literacy learners already have many basic reading skills. These learners have progressed beyond the "learning to read" stage to the level of "reading to learn." Such learners often improve dramatically from simply being in a learning environment filled with positive and interesting experiences with the written word. For learners with virtually no reading skills, and there are many of these as well, basic reading is a major goal of their program, and structured instruction may be necessary. But who says that sequential instruction can't be interesting, fun, and for that matter, thematic? Local communities can develop structured sequential materials that reflect learner themes. Or they can develop their own thematic materials that complement a more generalized basic skills primer. Publishers can develop sequential primers that aren't so generic. Such materials can reflect themes often expressed by typical learner populations, such as domestic violence, discrimination, unemployment, transportation, welfare issues, housing issues, and the problems of assimilation in a second culture.

A core of sequential skills instruction can be supplemented by a variety of learner-generated or issue-based materials that may or may not be absolutely consistent with the skills already taught. The treatment of learner-generated themes and dialogue will probably generate vocabulary, grammar, and sounds that go beyond the narrow confines of skills already treated. But since the sequence of skills selected was an arbitrary, imperfect choice in the first place, activities that develop critical thinking and provide motivation can only contribute to the success of the instruction. Trust the learner-guided process to yield unexpected but very positive alterations.

In your mix of materials, don't underestimate your capacity and the capacity of learners to generate meaningful educational experiences. You and your co-learners have access to a local reality that the most skillful linguists and publishers don't have. "Good" materials may consist of several learning activities and materials rather than a single primer. And with all this concern for reading basics, don't forget critical thinking skills and problem-posing dialogue, cultural celebration, and community action to solve problems as key elements in the mix of literacy materials.

In this debate, Ms. Mix thought she had the last word, but she doesn't. I do. And my last word to Ms. Mix is "amen." Effective programs consciously choose the mix of methods and materials that is most appropriate to the needs and goals of their learners. Laubach-sponsored programs throughout Latin America have produced a diversity of sequential reading primers. All of these primers teach Spanish to beginning readers in sequential fashion, but each book was developed around local issues. Therefore, each book begins with different key words and presents a sequence of reading skills that varies from the others. Each of these primers is further balanced by a number of local learning activities, supplemental and postliteracy materials, and various local forums for dialogue, cultural expression, and action. Two other examples—from Haiti and Bangladesh—illustrate a range of possibilities.

Village issues: Haiti

"What do you see in this picture?"

Women of the remote community of Hinche, Haiti, answer this question as they examine an illustration in their literacy primer. The simple drawing depicts a Haitian mother in a hut. She is standing by the bed of her obviously sick daughter and feeling the child's forehead. Printed on the adjoining page is the French Creole word for sickness, *maladi.*

Underneath this key word and on the following four pages are simple reading and writing exercises that help learners combine the various vowel and consonant sounds found in the word *maladi.* The facilitator begins the lesson with this drawing and asks several questions which lead to dialogue about causes, effects, and possible solutions related to sickness and health care in the learners' lives. Typical dialogue questions connected to this picture are, "Have you experienced sickness like this in your home?" "What do you think the causes of this sickness are?" "What kind of health care do we have in our zone?"

"What steps (concerning sanitation and nutrition, for example) can we take in our homes to reduce sickness?" "How can we organize to improve health care in our zone?"

This discussion is followed by a folk ballad about a mother whose child dies from an untreated illness.

The Haitian lesson involves the sequential treatment of basic reading skills. It also deals with the issues that emerge from dialogue and song, and generates possible action steps to address these issues. Lessons begin with a picture and key words that have powerful social and political meaning for the participants—*market, woman, justice, hunger, work.* These words are not only the thematic basis for problem-posing dialogue and eventual organization for action, they are also presented sequentially, in order for participants to learn basic sounds and combinations. Each subsequent chapter builds upon the skills of the previous lessons to teach increasingly more difficult and complex reading skills.

Cultural expression: Bangladesh

By the red glow of three *harikan* (hurricane) lanterns, twenty-three men sit on bamboo mats crowded on the dirt floor of a tiny hut. Each man holds a thin booklet, and in the dim light stares at the words on the page. At the facilitator's call, all begin reading aloud. Each reader is at a different point in the text. Some even read from different books. All the readers speak in chant-like cadences and rock their heads gently back and forth in rhythm with their words. At that very moment, in 103 other village sites throughout the rural Shibpur district of Bangladesh, identical scenes take place as groups of men and women gather for nightly literacy sessions.

The exercise reflects a thoughtful decision about basic reading curriculum made by leaders of this literacy-for-social-change program. In years past, the group had experimented with two different sets of reading primers, one that emphasized village themes, and another that focused solely on linguistic skills in the Bengali language. The program had some success with both materials, but leaders found that learners in their particular district were most involved when they used primers based on their strong Moslem cultural heritage.

The program coordinator explained, "The people have heard these prayers and poems sung since birth. Now, to actually read these verses, they are so excited." The culturally-based introduction to reading is working well. Enrollment and attendance is close to 100 percent of the village adults, who come faithfully six evenings per week.

At the same time, the participants are also actively involved in community action and problem solving as part of the program. In a mutual learning and action effort, they are digging new wells, improving their homes damaged in recent floods, planting forests, starting health programs, and launching successful cooperative income-generating projects. Graduates of the culturally-based basic reading and writing primers move on to postliteracy learning that further emphasizes basic skills, critical thinking, and action, using materials focused on community issues.

Facilitators acknowledge that their basic primers don't deal directly with critical thinking or community action, and except for their relevant cultural content, are minimally adequate in teaching basic skills. But participants move from the primers to other materials and activities. The net result over an extended time frame is balanced integration of all the literacy-for-social-change components.

Creating an effective learning mix

To achieve an effective mix of literacy methods and materials, leaders must consider a range of different variables—learner goals and needs, primers and supplementary materials (home-grown, purchased, or both), postliteracy materials, available resources and facilities, possible learning and action exercises, and the desired balance of fundamental skills, cultural expression, critical thinking, and action. Each program must develop its own mix of these variables.

The list of learning activities that follows is not a substitute for the decisions each program must make about its own blend of methods and materials, but a sample of successful techniques and exercises used by programs in many countries. Many of them can be used in a group setting or in one-to-one tutoring. Alone, they don't constitute a comprehensive program for teaching reading and writing. As creative triggers for selecting or developing a total reading program, they do illustrate ways in which learner goals can be identified and incorporated in a learning curriculum that integrates all four components of literacy for social change.

Brainstorming. This group activity begins with an open-ended question that provokes thought, but has no right or wrong answers. All responses are written on newsprint or a blackboard. Some examples of brainstorming questions are: "What do you see in this picture?" "How do you think the character felt in the story we just read?" "Why do you think the mayor has adopted such a policy?" After writing all the responses, the facilitator asks, "Which of these belong together? How would you group them?" One or all of these participant-generated headings are written on the side of the blackboard as the basis for further discussion, writing exercises, or lessons in sight vocabulary.

Key word exercises. This exercise, another group activity, invites participants to develop thematic vocabulary lists. Start with directions such as, "List five words that are keys to raising children," or "List six words that describe life in our neighborhood." The process of selecting the most important words for inclusion in a limited-number list helps participants develop analytical and group decision-making skills. The completed list can be used for discussion, writing exercises, or vocabulary development.

Language experience. Language experience is a very popular method for enabling learners to share an experience or concern orally and then deal with the account in written form. Typically, the learner recounts an experience, and the facilitator/tutor or other learners record the story on paper, cassette tape, or on the blackboard. Depending on skill level, the originator of the story may also participate in writing down the oral account. The story in written form becomes the basis for reading, dialogue, vocabulary lessons, and even lessons in grammar, sentence structure, spelling, or other language arts. There are many variations of this basic technique. The process can involve one or many learners. It can involve one sentence or a very long manuscript. One variation involves students picking out the most meaningful words in the experience story. These words are written on cards which the learners match to the story or use to create new stories.

Oral histories. One very effective combination of brainstorming, key word exercises, and language experience comes from the multicultural curriculum of the Lutheran Settlement House Women's Program in Philadelphia. The program has developed a process for obtaining oral histories from learners, beginning with the brainstorming question, "What do you think about when you think about the lives of your parents (or grandparents or an older relative or friend)?" Responses are listed on the blackboard, and learners group these responses by common themes or headings. A key word exercise follows with the question, "When you look at these headings, what one word can you think of that would sum up or best describe your parents' or grandparents' lives?" One-word responses are listed on the blackboard. Students then write or speak into a tape recorder in response to the question, "What is it about your parents'/grandparents' lives that made you come up with this key word?" Further questions may be needed to elicit further information.

The taped responses are transcribed word-for-word and edited for grammar. Spelling and grammar are corrected in the written stories. The oral histories become the basis for class reading, discussion, and language arts lessons.

Cloze exercises. Cloze exercises involve reading passages with certain words omitted. These exercises can be used for many purposes. As a tool for strengthening reading comprehension, every n^{th} word may be deleted; the learner fills in the blanks. Alternatively, the facilitator may delete only certain key words to elicit learner discussion or practice in vocabulary development.

Another equally valid focus can be the learners' relationship with the ideas expressed in writing. For example, a cloze exercise could be used to stimulate reflection and discussion on issues of importance to learners, such as domestic violence. Simple sentences could be used. "Dad hit the kid with a __________ . The kid __________ her lip." More difficult vocabulary can also be applied. "When the baby starts screaming, his mother feels __________ . She wants to __________ ." Learners can select the type of words that would fit in without necessarily having one correct response for each missing word. They can also discuss the meaning of the passage and its possible application to their own lives.

Free writing. This technique encourages learners to express themselves freely in writing. Frequently, students are intimidated by the need for neatness, spelling, grammar, or what they think the teacher wants. Free writing is concerned only with free expression. The writer doesn't worry about grammar, punctuation, spelling, sentence structure, or anything that could interfere with the flow of thought. Learners can keep journals for free writing. Journal entries can be used for dialogue among learners or between learners and facilitators/tutors.

Mini-stories. This exercise may be dictated and transcribed like a language experience, or written by the learner. The mini-story is an incomplete sentence which the learner finishes with one phrase or a few sentences. Here are some examples. "Last year my family . . ." "This neighborhood needs . . ." "When my children get sick I . . ." "This morning I . . ." "I feel bad when . . ." "At Christmas we like to . . ." "The best thing that has happened in our community recently is . . ." "When there's no money in the house, I . . ."

Issue- or life-mapping. This activity can be completed in forty-five minutes or take as long as five entire days. In the center of a large blackboard or very large bulletin board covered with blank newsprint, draw a small box that represents a geographic starting place. Typically, that site is the place where the learners are currently gathered for class. For example, if the site were a neighborhood center, the facilitator would write the name of the center at the side of the square. On the top of the blank map the word *north* is written; on the bottom, *south;* then *east* on the right and *west* on the left.

From this point, important locations are placed in their geographic relationship to each other. Each of the learners' houses or apartments can be represented by a small square with a "roof" on top and the learner's name at the side. Key locations in the learners' lives are plotted and labeled. Locations might be: churches (a square with a cross on top) or mosques, schools, clinics, key roads, markets, bus stops, recreational areas, train stations, welfare facilities, a landowner's home, police or military facilities, employment sites, reservation boundaries, or other important sites. The map becomes a very individualized sketch of the places that the learners view as important in their lives. It reflects their view of the community.

The labels on the map develop sight word vocabulary. But the map itself and the relationship of certain sites provide a basis for lively dialogue that can lend itself to problem posing. For example, the facilitator might note, "I see that you live here, but the market (or clinic or job site) is way over there. How do you get to the market? What kind of transportation do you have? Does this transportation arrangement make it hard for you to get where you need to go?" Any number of learner issues and concerns can emerge from such a map. "How much are the rents in your neighborhood? What does housing cost in this higher-rent area? Why are people in this other neighborhood able to afford higher housing costs?" Extended use of the map can be the basis for introducing many problem-solving efforts as well as a rich variety of reading and writing exercises.

Problem-posing praxis. Derived from the writings of Paulo Freire, this enables learners to systematically define and analyze problems in their local and extended environment. Learners identify problems, effects, causes, and possible responses to concerns they feel are important. This activity, which can take anywhere from two to eight hours, can be applied in a variety of formats. Typically, the facilitator will ask participants to name community problems they think are important. Learners will name several problems, which are listed on an easel or chalkboard. By consensus or vote, the group selects one of these problems to discuss in that given session. Other problems can be treated at subsequent sessions. Learners then list what they believe are the effects of the problem. Each response is written down. After effects are listed, the participants identify causes and possible solutions. Learner responses are listed and can serve not only as the basis for dialogue, but also for reading and writing exercises.

Thematic photos, illustrations, and collages. Photos or illustrations that reflect the reality of learners' lives are excellent tools for generating dialogue as well as lessons in reading and writing. Such items can serve as the basis for generating key vocabulary, experience stories, free writing, brainstorming sessions, and other exercises. Key vocabulary lists readily lend themselves to lessons in such language components as phonetic sounds, prefixes, and suffixes.

Affinity groups and conversation circles. Small groups often encourage a level of discussion and expression not always possible in larger classes. Teams of learners can often generate stories, skits, or written positions on issues that enable individual participants to play a more active role with the support and collaboration of peers. Frequently, a small group project will enable a peer-tutoring process to emerge.

Photonovels and scrapbooks. In individual or small group projects, learners can express issues or cultural experiences through photography or scrapbook collections that are labeled with captions or descriptive paragraphs written by the learners. Creative learners can enhance stories with drawings or photos of their own.

Games and puzzles. Hangman, bingo, crossword puzzles, riddles, issue-oriented simulation games, and a host of commercially developed learning games provide fertile ground for reading and writing. If the vocabulary is also related to thematic issues being discussed by the learning group, then learners see these fun activities as also very relevant.

Book clubs and reading circles. Learners gather for the specific purpose of reading together or discussing what they have read.

Generally, the group reads the same book or article individually or together, and participants discuss their ideas and feelings about what they have read. Groups meet weekly, twice a month, or once a month.

Music. Students can learn and perform songs. Lyrics are a great source for vocabulary and dialogue. Facilitators can teach and reinforce reading and pronunciation skills with jingles, "raps," or rhythmic jazz chants. Participants can read or sing along with recorded music. Learners can compose their own songs and "raps." A learning group can put on its own talent show.

Skits and plays. Simple skits and plays, whether developed by learners, facilitators, or others, can raise issues for problem solving as well as develop basic skills. Learners read and write scripts and labels for props, engage in discussion about their reactions to presentations, and use the presentations and discussions as springboards for further writing.

Street walks. In Canada, Toronto's Beat the Streets literacy program uses the learners' home turf as a vocabulary source. In street walks (or rides) learners read the signs and captions of their neighborhood and talk about their lives there. Similar excursions in stores can yield functional reading vocabulary and discussions about neighborhood and consumer issues. Learners can even simulate a store or marketplace and recreate the literacy and math-related issues they encounter when buying or selling goods.

Newspapers and magazines. Virtually every section of a newspaper or magazine is a ripe source for stimulating discussion. Reading lessons can range from identifying words and reading headlines and ads to critical discussion of articles.

Newsletters and bulletin boards. Writings and experience stories by learners can be posted on bulletin boards or published in simple newsletters. Student writings can be compiled and copied in a single collection. A collaborative history or issue booklet can be developed by the entire learning group.

Arts, crafts, and hobbies. Whatever creative forum the learners enjoy or can share is a great avenue for reading and writing instruction. Painting, drawing, quilting, sewing, cake decorating, rock collecting, cooking, home remedies, astrology, mechanics, fishing—any of these has the built-in potential to generate written labels, language experience, key words, and other related exercises.

United States

Instruction in fundamental skills is an integral component of the literacy-for-social-change model wherever in the world the program might be.

India

Africa

Philippines

Haiti

Chapter 8
Critical thinking

Eight leaders of the Chumash tribe outside Santa Barbara, California, gathered under a backyard shade tree. They were preparing to become facilitators for a literacy program among their own people. Seated in a circle on the grass, they looked at a large photograph depicting several people watching television. Throughout the day, this simple photograph served as the focal point for a stimulating training experience based upon a process of dialogue. In this context, dialogue is much more than simple conversation or a scripted vocabulary lesson. It is an exchange of ideas and feelings focused on an issue or experience. It involves directed questioning and discussion regarding specific focal points of shared concern.

As prospective facilitators, their experience that day was nearly identical to the process through which they would later lead other learners from the tribe. A similar pattern of dialogue is an important element of literacy learning among many other groups in the United States and worldwide.

The purpose of this dialogue is to develop those skills and attitudes known as critical thinking or critical consciousness. The critical thinker not only deciphers information, but also examines, analyzes, and questions it. A critical thinker is not a passive recipient of knowledge, but an active agent who uses information as a tool for solving problems and creating new perspectives.

Some educators are skeptical of any education process, such as dialogue, that professes to promote higher-level skills before learners have mastered all the fundamentals. They insist that gaps in lower-level foundation skills will prevent learners from acquiring higher skills. Others counter by noting that daily living constantly requires learners to respond to realities that aren't defined by controlled, sequential skill levels. They suggest that when learners interact with real-life issues through a process such as dialogue, the dynamic learning context generates motivation to achieve, retain, and apply skills and information. Participants read and speak to understand and convey meaning, and the process accelerates all learning.

Literacy-for-social-change programs don't choose between fundamental skills and critical thinking. They integrate both, along with cultural expression and action projects. In many effective programs, learners attend sessions that emphasize fundamental skills, while also participating in other groups primarily intended to develop higher-level skills and consciousness. Learning activities aimed at developing fundamental skills can simultaneously strengthen critical thinking. And exercises aimed at critical thinking can incorporate fundamental skills instruction. As always, the ideal is to find an appropriate, integrated balance.

A successful dialogue experience stimulates the capacity for critical thinking. Dialogue is by no means the only way to generate critical thinking, but it is one very effective and widely recognized approach.

Any number of events and forums can generate dialogue. In literacy programming, the process is typically initiated with a photograph, illustration, paragraph, story, skit, or some other form of expression that reflects an important reality from the learners' lives. These symbols from the learners' experience "codify," in Freire's terms, some dimension of the learners' world. By identifying, analyzing, and questioning the contents of this "code" of reality, learners "decode," or "read" the issues of their lives. Participants attain heightened understanding of the effects, causes, and solutions of the problems of day-to-day living. They can examine these problems from local, state, regional, national, and international perspectives. And they can act to bring about desirable change.

Dialogue to develop critical thinking lends itself very effectively to reading lessons. Michael James describes the effective facilitator as a "choreographer" who artfully balances a range of concerns—issues, individuals, perspectives, priorities, and reading skill development—within the framework of the dialogue experience.

The best codes tend to be culturally unique to the learning group involved. Their value often diminishes when applied to culturally dissimilar groups. A picture that is extremely provocative among learners in Bangladesh will elicit little response from Filipino learners.

Occasionally, a code will have more universal appeal. This is true of the code used by the Chumash group. This particular photograph, or an illustration like it, has been used in settings throughout Latin America and the United States. It depicts several persons watching television in what appears to be a humble home setting. (See photo on pages 92-93.)

Raúl Añorve, a facilitator in an experimental project linking Laubach Literacy International, California Literacy, Inc., and the Irvine Foundation, often uses this photo as a model for training prospective facilitators in a statewide network of neighborhood-based organizations. The photo has appeal because all of the California groups he has worked with—Native Americans, Latinos, African Americans, Filipinos, Indo-Chinese, Polynesians, and Anglos—tend to have television sets and can identify with a family setting. This is true even in many developing nations where television often finds its way into the dirt-floor shacks of the poor.

This photo can serve as a useful example of the dynamics of the dialogue process, which includes several phases: identification of the code, application to personal experience, values clarification, generation of key thematic words, analysis, reflection, and solutions. Readers are invited to consider their own ideas and opinions about television in following the process.

Identification of the code

"What do you see in this picture?"

An effective dialogue process moves through several levels of participation. The first is the identification phase. This step may seem obvious, but it is an important beginning point —identifying the basic elements of the code. It begins with a question such as, "What's being said in the paragraph we just read?" or, "What happened in the skit we just saw?" For the TV picture, the question is simple. "What's happening in this photograph?" or even better, "What do you see in this photograph?" Learners are invited to name what they see in the photo.

Responses from a group of participants typically start out with a statement like, "There are six people watching TV." Another participant comments, "It's a family." The facilitator then probes further, asking, "Why do you say it's a family?" An answer might be, "There's an older person and there are the children." Many will comment on what program the family might be watching, or what the ages of the children might be, or how far apart the individuals are seated from each other.

Courtesy Mexican Government, Instituto Nacional Educación Adultos

Occasionally, the facilitator asks further questions to keep comments moving. "What kind of furnishings are in the home?" "What can you tell about the income of the people in the picture?"

Often, observers will deduce a number of problems in the photograph, such as, "It feels so cold. Everybody's isolated and away from each other. It's like the TV's keeping them apart." The intense focus on the contents of this single photograph draws people into the scene. It soon becomes apparent that the commonplace scenes of life often involve a lot more than is noted at first glance.

Application

"Does your family watch TV?"

After the participants have helped identify objects in the scene, the facilitator begins to ask questions that enable learners to apply the scene to their own lives. For example, "Does your family watch TV?" or, "Does your family have a TV similar to the one in the picture?" Most participants do watch TV and answer affirmatively. Further questions provoke thoughtful responses. "What kinds of programs do you watch?" or, "How many hours a day do you watch TV?" If possible, every participant should answer these questions. The respondents' names and part or all of their responses can be written on a chalkboard or on newsprint. Writing learners' comments helps focus discussion.

Participants might mention the news, adventure shows, sports, movies, cultural events, and soap operas. They may identify specific programs they like. They may mention watching videos, prompting further questions by the facilitator such as, "Do you have a VCR?" "What are the advantages and disadvantages of a VCR?" "What kinds of movies do you watch?" The learners' responses can lead the facilitator to probe deeper with questions like, "What time of day or what days of the week do you most enjoy watching TV?" "Which kinds of sports do you enjoy most?" "Does the situation in the picture seem real to you?" "Is it similar to your own life?"

Values clarification

"Why do you like to watch those programs?"

Each participant should respond to a question like, "Why do you like watching the programs you listed?" Their answers are a reflection of their values. They have to ponder these responses and do a little soul searching.

Participants' answers can often be summarized with words like *entertainment, relaxation,* or *information.* These words may be listed on the chalkboard as well. Frequently, their responses will be very individualized. "I watch football on TV because my husband likes to watch sports." The facilitator continues to probe the learners' values. "What is it about soap operas that you enjoy?" "Why do you like news programs more than movies?"

At this and every phase of the dialogue process, the facilitator must be highly sensitive to the comments and interests of the learners. The leader is seeking to identify key themes that truly reflect the feelings of a majority of participants. The direction of the process is shaped by the questions asked. The facilitator's biases or the views of one or two outspoken participants can direct the dialogue in ways that don't reflect the interests of the entire group. For example, one facilitator might feel strongly that soap operas are a waste of time. He or she might attempt to focus the group's attention on soap operas instead of pursuing a theme of broader interest to the group.

With profound respect for the learners and their concerns, the facilitator should try to keep the process moving without controlling its outcome and thereby stifling the sense of participation and shared ownership. By directing the process with too heavy a hand, the facilitator can deny learners the opportunity to develop the analytical and synthesizing skills that are essential goals of the experience.

Generating key thematic words

"What's the real issue here?"

At this point in the dialogue, sensitivity in interpreting the interests of the group is crucial. The facilitator isn't bound to keep the group talking about the photograph or even about TV. A major purpose of all the preceding dialogue and such intense use of the photograph is to draw the participants into a critical examination of some aspect of their lives. That examination will probably keep the discussion focused on television issues. But the focus may also change.

For example, in one group, the discussion started with a focus on TV news. The facilitator asked a learner, "What types of news programs do you enjoy most?" The participant quickly answered with an example of a report he had seen recently about drugs in the area. Another mentioned a similar documentary she had seen on drugs. People enthusiastically began talking about drugs and how deeply threatened they feel by drugs in their neighborhood. It became very clear that the group wanted to talk about the drug problem far more than they wanted to talk about TV programs. The facilitator wisely decided to follow the interest of the group. However, one learner still wanted to talk about TV sports. The leader linked the two interests with the question, "Do any sports figures use drugs?" The subject returned to drugs, the topic of greatest concern to the group.

The theme of the session is generated by the group. For the group above, the key thematic word was obviously *drugs*. For most groups using the TV photo, the word will probably be *television*. In fact, any number of key words could emerge from a dialogue beginning with the TV picture. That word becomes a focal point—a powerful, memorable symbol of the more complicated reality the group has been discussing.

Analysis

"What makes a good program or a bad program?"

As participants agree on the name of the issue (drugs, television, or whatever), the discussion has reached the point where the learners' already stated values on the issue can be examined. The facilitator may ask any number of questions to provoke analysis: "What makes a good television program?" "We've talked about TV news as a source of information. How reliable a source of information is television?" "What are other sources of information and how reliable are they compared with television?" "What is entertaining?" "Is TV news (entertainment, sports, etc.) part of your family's communication pattern?" "How does TV affect your life (your family, your community, the nation)?" "Does TV help us or hurt us?" "What about violence on TV?" "Does TV teach our children values? What do you think of these values?" "How does TV affect elections (crime, public policies, etc.)?" "What is the main purpose of TV broadcasting—to make money or to serve the public interest?"

Questions like these will elicit a wide range of responses and stories from the learners' experiences. As a result, learners may express very specific needs for change, such as, "Members of our family/neighborhood need to find ways to spend more time talking with each other." "We need to learn about the candidates in other ways besides television." "I'm concerned about how violent my children are with each other." "I need to get more control over how I spend my time."

Reflection

"What has happened?"

This whole process takes time, and the facilitator must also be a time manager. An effective dialogue session is usually at least two-and-a-half hours. It may even involve two or three days of class time. Ideally, the process should end with a period of reflection—a time when options and commitment for action can be discussed. The facilitator may say something like, "Let's reflect on what we have just discussed. What have we talked about as a group? What has happened? Let's look at the different ways that we've viewed this problem. How have our positions been in agreement with each other? Where have we had differences of opinion?" This reflective discussion is likely to generate statements of summary, reminders of key issues and ideas, further values clarification and analysis, statements of what remains undone, and an affirmation that learning has taken place. It is an evaluative moment and sets the stage for subsequent dialogue and action. It is best if the same group can engage in several similar sessions involving a variety of issues.

Solution/action

"What can we do?"

The final round of questions deals with possible solutions. The facilitator should ask, "What can we do as a group to address the problems we've talked about today?" "How can we organize ourselves for action?" "What can you do as an individual or family?" Typical responses include modifying TV viewing patterns, initiating strategies for improved family or neighborhood interaction, seeking alternative sources of information and entertainment, and forming recreation groups.

The example of dialogue emerging from the television photo is one model that can be applied to an almost infinite variety of issues. The model can be modified. Phases of the dialogue process can be shortened or even dealt with in isolation. More importantly, the model has flexible application. Codes can depict poor housing, unemployment, domestic violence, racism, sexism, transportation problems, hunger, exploitation at the marketplace, health problems, land tenure questions, credit problems, celebratory themes, and virtually any other learner-generated issues.

More formats for generating dialogue

Many potential formats exist for generating dialogue. They all can help learners in the quest for critical thinking skills and attitudes. In the few examples that follow, all of the dialogue phases (such as identification, and values clarification) can be developed. All the formats require a facilitator to ask thought-provoking and probing questions.

The problem-posing praxis: Learners list problem areas and select one for in-depth discussion. In discussion they identify and list the effects of this problem, its causes, possible solutions, and what might result from those solutions.

Taking a stand: This activity presents the learners with a hypothetical problem and describes the course that some individual or group took to solve the problem. Participants are asked, "Do you agree or disagree?" If they agree, they stand at one end of the room. If they disagree, they stand at the other. If they abstain or partially agree, then they stand closer to the middle. Participants must explain why they stand where they do, and defend their positions. As they hear other arguments, they may physically move to reflect their changing understanding of the issue.

Issue-mapping: Learners plot life realities on a map. (See page 83.)

Drawing the reality: Participants divide into very small groups (of three to four) and draw their understanding of a given situation. Their drawing can be in the form of symbols or a story. Some activities ask participants to draw the problem as a symbolic creature or form of transportation. Participants label their drawings, and then describe them to the larger group.

Imaging: In small groups, learners draw, describe, or even act out their shared image of what the future regarding a specified issue ought to be. They create an image of the future that involves their concept of changed relationships and conditions. Their notion of possible solutions thus becomes very concrete as they talk about what actions it would take to make their image a reality.

Circle within a circle: Participants are divided equally into two groups and each group forms a circle, one within the other. As music plays or clapping takes place, the two circles move around in opposite directions until the music stops. One person from each circle now faces a person from the other circle. For five or ten minutes each pair discusses one question. Then the circles reconvene, the music starts again, new pairings are formed, and a new question is presented for discussion. Finally, these questions and the process are discussed by the group as a whole.

Integrating basic skills

Any stage in the dialogue process can be used for a reading or writing lesson. How this works depends on a lot of factors, many of which the facilitator controls, some of which cannot be controlled. The specific learning needs and goals of the group members and their purpose for meeting are the most important factors. If, for instance, the group consists of people who have a mixed range of reading skills, those who read well may find a lengthy treatment of reading sounds connected to the key word *television* a tedious interruption. A group of low-level readers, who expect to learn reading and writing basics, may find the connection of skill learning with dialogue to be useful.

In any case, the facilitator should strive to balance basic reading/writing skill development with the flow of dialogue. Given the key word *television,* the facilitator might approach the task with questions like, "What one word would you choose to express what we've been talking about?" "How do you spell the word *television?*" "What does the word mean?" "Some of its parts give us a good clue; what is the first part of the word?" "Does this sound, 'tele,' appear in any other words you can think of (telephone, telescope, telegraph)?" "What do you think this sound (syllable, prefix, root) means?" The learners can also identify the key consonant or vowel sounds of the word. Learners can be invited to use the word in a sentence or story.

The dialogue techniques cited in this chapter offer a few samples to generate thinking. There are a host of possible applications of these techniques and principles in a variety of group or even one-to-one settings. Dialogue is not the only tool for developing critical thinking skills, although it is one of the best.

The alternatives for integrating basic skills and critical thinking instruction are limitless. Similarly, forms of critical thinking such as analysis, reflection, or problem posing have a direct relationship with cultural expression and action. Critical thinking is a vital component of literacy-for-social-change programs, for without critical consciousness and skills, genuine individual and community change is not possible.

Chapter 9

Celebrating culture

A Chinese folktale speaks of a wise but ailing father who knew that his days on earth would soon end. He gathered sons, daughters, and grandchildren around his deathbed to pass on to them his final legacy. He looked lovingly upon his descendants and spoke with emotion.

"I am poor and I have little treasure to bestow. Even so, I have thought much about this matter, and I do have great gifts for you, if you are ready to claim them.

"First, I give you the prayer of our ancestors. But you must know, it will not become yours until you say it. I give you this treasured scroll, the history of our generations. But it is not yours until you read it. And I give you the songs of our people. They, too, are not yours until you sing them. Even the treasures of your heart, which you have gained through your life in our home, are not really yours until you express them."

The wealth of a wise and loving father rested in song, prayer, and history—the most valued prizes he knew. But these most treasured gifts could not be bestowed until the receiver gained ownership through expression.

Literacy is expression. It is active. It involves listening, speaking, reading, and writing—not just to gain information, but also to exercise our humanity, both individually and collectively. Such expression is the essence of culture. The celebration of culture is not just a pleasant adjunct to a reading lesson. The fundamentals of reading and writing may be the skeleton of literacy education, and critical thinking its flesh, but cultural expression is the heart.

Music, dance, and other forms of cultural expression are the heart of literacy-for-social-change programs in Mexico, *above,* India, *below,* and throughout the world.

A literacy worker among migrant workers in South Carolina once told me, "I figure that when people can say and write what they experience, what they feel, then they're really literate. When they tell their stories, sing their songs, or act out their hopes in a skit, it's as much a literacy lesson as covering phonics or spelling."

Cultural expression brings meaning, a feeling of shared identity, and a sense of fun to those who are learning to read and write. Expression through music, storytelling, art, drama, poetry, and dance can also be very effective devices for teaching specific reading and writing skills. Reading and writing the words of a song which a learning group then sings develops many literacy skills, as do writing and performing a skit, voicing one's life story, weaving a ceremonial cloth, or organizing a village heritage dance. Cultural expression stimulates learner participation and enhances learners' capacity to remember.

In the literacy-for-social-change model, cultural expression is an integral part of the total process. It is both a means to, and an end of, literacy learning. It shares an equally important role with fundamental skills, critical thinking, and action projects.

In Colombia's Atlantic coast region, for example, thirty-eight villages of destitute, landless *campesinos*, working with the Laubach center for Adult Education in Medellín, have initiated a large-scale, literacy-for-social-change project involving some forty thousand participants. Typical wages paid to farm workers in these impoverished communities are equivalent to $2.50 (American dollars) per day. These wages aren't enough to feed the workers' families or provide housing or health care.

In this setting, the literacy program is a life-or-death issue. In every village, the program includes education in fundamental skills, critical thinking, and community projects to generate income and improve health. These are obvious survival matters, but every village program also considers cultural expression to be an equally important component. Each learning site maintains an active popular culture committee that promotes indigenous dance, music, and drama as part of the learning program. Sometimes, the cultural expression takes place as a separate event. Frequently, however, it is woven into a basic reading lesson or a community productivity project. Cultural expression strengthens and complements all forms of literacy learning.

Misyon Alfa, a national literacy campaign sponsored by the Catholic Diocese in Haiti, also bases its learning activities in cultural roots. The learning materials reflect cultural and social themes of the people. Learners in numerous rural communities and urban centers experience a mix of cultural and linguistic instruction, including song, dance, social issues, phonics, spelling, and sight vocabulary. Aptly, their Creole-language literacy primer is called *Goute Sel,* a "taste of salt." The metaphor comes from two cultural sources—the Bible's reference to "the salt of the earth," and voodoo tradition which identifies salt as a powerful element for raising "zombies" from the dead. In Haitian culture, salt symbolizes that which is basic to life as well as resurrection and new life. Literacy learning points the way to a new life as well.

Effective literacy programs in the United States and worldwide have likewise found that "a taste of salt"—namely, cultural activity, is an essential ingredient in a successful learning process. And the best source of cultural materials for incorporation in the learning process is the learners themselves. The best stories are stories from their life experience; the best music is drawn from their cultural milieu.

Literacy lessons in Lalbandi, Nepal, regularly include the singing of religious and cultural chants. Adult students in a Fontana, California, English-as-a-second-language program share Samoan food, traditional dance, native art, and Polynesian quilting as part of their literacy learning. East African facilitators teach a basic health and literacy lesson with a popular song they renamed "Brush the Flies from Baby's Eyes." Learners in Ajoya, a remote village in west Mexico, developed a skit with talking animals and peasant characters to express their feelings about their farms. In Dulce, New Mexico, the literacy classroom is lined with paintings and baskets created by the adult students. Learners in the Andes of Ecuador collaborate to create their own homemade photonovels about life in their region.

Puppet theater depicting the life of local residents stimulates learning and discussion in central Mexico's village of San Telmo de Roa. The Chumash Indians near Santa Barbara, California, resisted adult literacy instruction until they recognized that the classes would be a way for the traditional legends of the tribal elders to be recorded and passed on to the next generation. In Brooklyn, New York, learners strengthen literacy skills by composing and performing rhythmic and rhyming "raps." In Viquí, Panama, learning groups collect and share local folk stories, recipes, home remedies, and songs. Sidewalk fences outside the Indian Center's bilingual learning program in Boston, Massachusetts, are covered with participant-created murals. A massive network of *campesino* educational programs in Colombia and Bolivia begins the learning process by creating community "cultural centers," which promote folk dance, learners' theater, art, and song. In Haripād, India, class frequently begins with traditional dances performed by the learners and their children.

The list of examples is virtually endless. They all illustrate cultural celebration as the lifeblood of literacy instruction. Moreover, among marginalized populations, whose cultural practices are generally treated as inferior by the dominant larger society, cultural expression is an absolutely crucial ingredient for program success. Cultural celebration as a foundation for all learning strengthens the participants' sense of self-worth and generates motivation.

"Secret" cultures

During the days of slavery in the United States, the master demanded respect. Slaves feigned deference, while maintaining a world of their own where a secret culture gave them some sense of dignity and control over their lives. Numerous records document a widespread practice of late-night clandestine literacy classes in the woods and sheds, and even hidden religious services. For those slaves who were caught, the penalties were severe, perhaps even fatal. But they braved the risk to preserve a level of cultural and individual integrity. It was a need as strong as physical survival.

For most of the poor today, there's no physical slavery. Yet many poor people still maintain a second culture, apart from the dominant mainstream culture in which they live. It too is a "secret" culture, not because it is deliberately hidden, as in the days of slavery, but because few in the dominant society care enough to discover, listen, and learn. All too often, education and development programs are aimed at replicating the technology and cultural values of a middle-class, Western world. More often than not, the institutions in charge convey indifference or even disdain for the participants' cultural perspective.

In many cases, educational programs, temporary training, inoculation campaigns, or building projects lead to no permanent improvement. In fact, they often do damage. For participants, the experience tends to be one more exercise in cultural humiliation and dependency. A mass campaign in Africa, for example, distributed foil packets filled with lifesaving fluid to thousands of mothers whose children suffered serious diarrhea related to malnutrition. The fluid could save children from dehydration and death. Unfortunately, mothers became convinced that in the future, the cure for their children's sickness must come from the outside, that they were incapable of helping themselves. Unable to get more foil packets, they gave in to the sickness and even the death of their children. They were never told that the lifesaving fluid in the packet was a solution of water, salt, and sugar. They could have easily made it themselves.

Well-meaning teachers or administrators may achieve short-term objectives such as test score gains, or some construction goal (usually at great expense), and declare their program a success. In 1982, European agency workers built a million-dollar irrigation system to save impoverished farmers in Ethiopia from drought. The program was proclaimed a great triumph, but three years later the once-fine canals lay in disrepair.

"We don't know how to fix them," explained a local farmer. "Besides, no one ever asked us if we wanted the system."

Lasting change among the poor isn't likely to happen through big capital projects or educational programs that are built upon the aspirations of outside planners. Genuine human development requires an educational process based upon the goals and aspirations of those in need.

The concept of learner-guided education underscores an important notion: Participants in education and development learn best within their own cultural perspective. In the process, facilitators or founders who come from the outside need to become educated in the strengths and richness of the previously "secret" culture of the participants. Such a process often tends to be a celebration of the participants' cultural view, which in turn sets a climate for effective learning and change.

A big, mean, modern world

Many would argue that this notion is flawed. As one development expert bluntly told me, "This idea only reinforces superstitions and attitudes that retard progress. People in the bush and slums can hide in quaint old traditions that may make them feel warm and fuzzy. But that won't make the big, mean, modern world out there go away. It's just prolonging the agony."

This particular critic does have one point. The big, mean, modern world won't go away. No matter how well-grounded people are in their own sense of cultural self-worth, they have to deal with the dominant outside society, with its full force of media, expanding technology, and overwhelming economic and political power. People may not welcome or want the middle-class, Western world, but they must come to grips with its existence and the relationship it has to their lives.

Given this reality, the long-term success of literacy and development efforts among the poor requires an approach not only based upon the learners' perspectives, but also incorporating the cultural realities of being a minority population within a broader dominant society. Education that bridges the two cultural realities is often referred to as bicultural.

In northern Kenya, for example, the nomad Gabbra tribe struggled to preserve its ancient cultural roots while its people were dying of starvation. Exacerbating their problems, the Gabbra were being cheated by traveling merchants who took advantage of their gentle and trusting ways.

The Gabbra were determined to learn to read and write their own dialect and to organize to address their problems. They sought outside technical assistance, and leaders from their own ranks were selected to be trained as facilitators. Through dialogue and interviews, key vocabulary from the culture and issues of Gabbra life were selected. These words and themes then became the basis for instruction and action. Their learning effort was bicultural. It emerged from their perspective, but kept an additional focus on their relationship to the outside society that dominates their economic lives.

With this framework, they organized a cooperative venture to transport their goats to Nairobi, where they would be sold at a much higher price. Before, they had been dependent upon greedy traveling traders for the sale of their animals. They began learning simple math and bookkeeping skills to keep track of their cooperative assets. They began learning Swahili, the national language, in order to bargain with strength in the Nairobi market. Through this bicultural literacy/development process they are dealing with their foes and new outside friends on their own terms.

Seizing the best of two cultural worlds is the aim of bicultural learning. It applies to peasants, *barrio* residents, *campesinos*, and inner-city dwellers anywhere. If the hungry and homeless and destitute of this world are to survive, prosper, and contribute, then their need to learn and to relate with the outside world from the context of their own cultural reality must be affirmed. And in the process, all segments of society, not just the poor, can learn and benefit from each other.

School in the jungle

Mindoro, Philippines

The Hanunuo Mangyan tribe, like other aboriginal groups in the Philippines and worldwide, is a native people displaced by powerful outsiders. A gentle, simple people, the Mangyans retreated from the encroachment of land-hungry colonizers to inaccessible jungle highlands. Lowland speculators looking for oil and profit continue to steal more of the Mangyans' homeland. These primitive people, who lack language and negotiation skills to deal with the sophisticated lowlanders, continue to lose. With no protective treaties, tensions are high.

The Mangyans feel even more threatened by a cultural attack from the lowlanders. Years ago, the Philippine government set up boarding schools far from the Mangyan homeland. By law, the children are separated from their villages for schooling where they learn the dominant national dress, culture, and language. Their home language is forbidden in the schools. They are taught that their "backward" tribal ways should be replaced by superior lowland attitudes and behavior. The real lessons are devastating. "You, your family, language, and whole way of life are inferior. You should be ashamed of who you are." To survive, children learn to give "correct," but humiliating required answers. Not surprisingly, only 2 percent of them graduate.

In lowland society, Mangyans are viewed as bumpkins who can't succeed. But the real damage is back home. Culturally disoriented, returning students are embarrassed by their parents' ways. Resulting conflicts tear families apart and divide the community. Young people drop out of school, leave home, and assume sub-class lives in lowland cities. Robbed of self-worth, this growing lost generation represents a whole new set of social problems in the Philippines.

Alarmed by the erosion of their families, "illiterate" highland parents took action. In spite of intense opposition that questioned the Mangyans' capacity to provide a "quality" education, the tribe won permission to start its own school. With only a minimal start-up grant, parents built a one-room facility by hand, hired a teacher, and took control of curriculum development. Children learned to read and write their own dialect. Mangyan art, music, dance, and agriculture based upon unique highland farming conditions and traditions were emphasized. The bicultural program also taught the Filipino national language and government-required subjects. Children learned information that would enable them to interact with the outside world while being grounded in their own culture. There were no dropouts, and the first class graduated. They are indeed getting the best of both worlds.

Inspired by the school's success, many parents stood outside and watched through the window to learn with their children. Parents formed their own program to learn to read and write Mangyan as well as the national language. This bicultural adult program emphasizes issues the Mangyans face in dealing with outside society, celebrates highland culture, and involves participants in action projects to fund their school.

Bicultural education for both cultures

Fort Duchesne, Utah

In the United States, Native American tribes such as the Ute in Utah face nearly identical issues. Ute reservation territory today has dwindled to a fraction of the area it covered before the white man took the land. Like the Mangyans, Ute children were taken from home to learn a "superior" culture and were punished for speaking Ute.

Bicultural education is a survival issue, and American Indians are striving to regain command of their cultural destiny. In 1983, the government boarding schools were closed, and Ute children are now bused daily to non-Indian public schools miles away. At first, they lagged five grade levels below white children, and 82 percent dropped out. With painfully slow progress, tribal leaders have struggled to have Ute heritage and language taught in the public schools. Now, the curriculum includes native culture as taught by Ute teachers. As a direct result, learning performance of Ute children rapidly improved, up an average of three grade levels.

Tribal leaders want to run their own schools someday. In the meantime, they enjoy the victory of seeing not only their children learn Ute ways, but also seeing white children learn Ute language, history, and culture. At first, white parents resisted, but now they see the benefits their children receive from this bicultural experience.

Like the Mangyans, Ute parents are inspired by their children's bicultural learning, an opportunity they were denied. Accordingly, adult interest in basic education, beginning with Ute language, traditions, and history, is mushrooming. They've just begun, but literacy learning in the best of two cultural perspectives is bringing new hope and vitality to the tribe.

Many tribal groups throughout the world have recognized the necessity of bicultural learning and have developed effective programs. The Purépecha tribe near Pátzcuaro, Mexico, for example, integrates bilingual Spanish and Purépecha literacy learning, native legends and heritage, and problem-solving activities in areas such as environment, health, and income.

Similarly, members of the Hualapai tribe in Peach Springs, Arizona, run their own educational programs for children and adults, using a curriculum they developed based on tribal traditions and customs. Literacy instruction is in Hualapai and English. Lucille Watahomigie, principal of the Peach Springs School, in describing the curriculum observed, "We don't accept the environmental disrespect and materialism we find outside. Our ancestors learned to live at peace with nature, and the white man could learn much from us."

Students learn, among other things, about Hualapai "ethnobotany." Learners experience the pragmatic and scientific as well as cultural aspects of Hualapai ways. Outdoor survival; harvest and preparation of prickly pear cactus; home production of nuts, butter, paint, glue, and medicine; waterproofing; and sundry lessons in biology, geology, history, wildlife management, and geography, are all a part of the unique Hualapai worldview. Learners gain the self-esteem as well as the information and skills necessary to deal with modern society.

The need for bicultural education is not limited to tribal groups. For tribal minorities, inner-city residents, or rural dwellers from Thailand to Toronto, the need for social and cultural affirmation is universal. All learners—and all segments of society—will benefit.

Two cultures blend in the Hualapai version of the Christmas story.
Courtesy Hualapai Bilingual Program

Chapter 10

Group action for problem solving

Louis was excited. He pointed down from the top of the slope toward the city of Port-au-Prince, Haiti.

"Look at that bird," he exclaimed. "That's a rare sight."

He explained that Port-au-Prince, with its lush tropical climate, has a remarkable lack of birds. In the city, winged creatures of all kinds have mostly disappeared. Children kill them with rocks, mothers strip the feathers, and the greasy prize is served with rice. A protein-rich meal like this is rare in a country where per capita income is less than $265 (American dollars) per year, and malnutrition and infant mortality are the norm.

Birds may be missing from the city, but in Haiti's countryside even the trees are gone. A resource-hungry populace has consumed hundreds of miles of once-lush forests. Trees are cut and consumed for charcoal to cook with or sell. Grazing animals eat even more foliage. Where rich forests once reigned, much of the countryside is now a barren desert. Without plant cover, the ground won't hold the topsoil. Little will grow, and what does grow requires increasing amounts of fertilizer, water, and labor.

If not reversed, this tragic cycle will lead to famine. Concerned development agencies are attempting to reforest Haiti's countryside to replenish the land. New trees are needed, but the effort is wasted as hungry people soon return to cut the trees for charcoal.

The problem of deforestation is not unique to Haiti. It is a global crisis. Each day the earth loses more acres of crop and forestland on every continent. The recurring famines in Ethiopia and the African Sahel are products of this same tragic cycle. As in Haiti, the real solution to the problem isn't simply to plant more trees.

The heart of the problem lies with the legitimate needs of people and their capacity for meeting those needs. Genuine development occurs when people are given the tools to meet these needs on an ongoing basis. Efforts to reforest the earth are doomed to long-term failure unless the people most directly affected by those forests are part of the solution. Like virtually all other issues of poverty and development, the problem begins and ends not with capital, technology, or even trees, but with people.

A human solution

Purūlia, West Bengal

Two hundred miles west of Calcutta, India, in the state of West Bengal, the problem of reforestation is being solved in a very human way. Several rural enclaves of landless people who survive by making and selling charcoal—those most often blamed for depleting the forests of the area—are replenishing the trees.

The remarkable effort involves volunteer scientists from Calcutta in collaboration with groups of the very poor and landless in the region near Purūlia. Here increasingly greater areas of once-rich forest are becoming barren and unproductive. During the flood season the unprotected topsoil is washed into rivers that eventually make their way into Calcutta. The city's sewers and streets get clogged with the unwelcome topsoil from the barren region. And with each passing year, successful farming in the region requires more water, fertilizer, and work.

Education helps people develop their own plans to solve their own problems.

School of Fundamental Research Forest Survival Project, West Bengal, India

For the sake of Calcutta and the Purūlia region, something had to be done to stop the disastrous cycle. A group of seven concerned scientists formed a private, voluntary development organization they call The School of Fundamental Research. Their first goal was to plant thousands of trees near Purūlia. Like the Haitians, they learned a sad lesson. As soon as the scientists planted trees, people would cut them down.

Undaunted, the scientists decided they would provide information to the people about the ecological damage caused by cutting the trees. They discovered that most of the people couldn't read the informational handouts, and those few who could read didn't understand all the technical jargon. They conducted street meetings to explain the facts, but their presentations were too academic to appeal to the people. Over a two-year period, they gradually stumbled onto a realization of what would really work. The people had to gain the capacity to understand the information, and also a sense of ownership, in order to change their behavior regarding the trees. Necessity taught the scientists the need for a learner-guided literacy process based upon the learners' cultural perspective and dialogue. People needed to develop basic skills, critical thinking, cultural expression, and action projects within the framework of their own needs and goals.

The scientists learned that the charcoal from the trees, though worth only pennies per day, was the people's sole livelihood. They couldn't survive without the charcoal. As the people gained new literacy skills and shared their mutual concerns with each other and the scientists, an interesting new perspective began to emerge.

The people began to realize that if all the trees were cut down, which would inevitably occur, they would then have absolutely no livelihood. They also began to learn from the scientists about some alternative forest products that didn't require the destruction of the forests. Sap from the lac tree could be sold for lacquer production; certain nuts and berries could be grown; even the large waxy leaves of certain trees could be sold as wrapping materials. Other crops could be grown around the trees. Management of the forests could allow for harvesting of dead trees and limbs and controlled cutting of live trees.

The education process took time, but out of the experience the people were able to develop their own plan and organization for solving the problem. They organized themselves into forest preservation committees. Each member had to plant 100 trees, and perform so many hours of guard duty each month to protect the new communal forest from outside poachers. In turn, each would have access to the controlled use of forest products. Committee members created this structure. They now have the knowledge, skills, and desire to keep enlarging the forest and managing this resource in a way that improves their livelihoods and saves the trees.

The people's literacy experience gave them motivation and capacity to bring about lasting change. This is because the development process finally centered on the people and not the trees. Their enthusiasm and success has since caught the interest of neighboring communities, which in turn have adopted the same successful process. And in the bordering countries of Nepal and Bangladesh, where the people confront similarly serious deforestation problems, participants in scores of literacy-for-social-change programs are also developing their own reforestation programs.

Reforestation is only one of a host of urgent development issues that agencies and groups throughout the world are trying to tackle. The principles that made the difference between success and failure in Purūlia are equally true for these other development efforts. The list of unresolved development challenges is overwhelming; hunger, housing, water, health care, transportation, income, livelihood, infant mortality, and the environment are just a few. Approaches that build upon the concerns, energy, and ideas of the people are the ones that will succeed in meeting these challenges. And these approaches tend to emphasize a learner-guided, bicultural educational process that integrates the fundamental skills of listening, speaking, reading, writing, and math with cultural expression, critical thinking, and community action.

Where do you begin?

Development is first an educational process. Once again, it's important to begin at the most obvious place. Start with the learners and their needs and goals. Trees, oral rehydration packets, vaccinations, improved housing, irrigation systems, roads, wells, or other improvements may be desperately needed. But when participants can identify these needs in a process of culturally relevant dialogue, they will more likely commit to a solution that they can support on a lasting basis. This process takes more time, but the long-term cost is much lower. After all, it is the people, not the outside agency, who must maintain and use the new developments in the future.

If the people don't feel strong ownership, then long-term failure is likely. When a new technology is simply imposed, they learn that "good" ideas must come from the outside. Thus they learn greater dependence and, if anything, are weakened in their capacity to initiate solutions to other problems. As soon as they face a maintenance problem or conflicting cultural norms, the new technology is abandoned.

The success of the Purūlia tree-preservation committee was not a fluke. Similar participant-initiated efforts are bringing about lasting change in settings throughout the world. The many community-oriented literacy projects described in this book have succeeded in enabling people to gain access to the skills, information, and attitudes necessary to organize and solve problems.

In Tinaja, Mexico, participants in a nine-year literacy-for-social-change effort sponsored by Laubach Literacy International drilled wells, built and maintained two aquaculture fish ponds, and established numerous poultry and goat projects, as well as a successful women's sewing cooperative and other income-generating initiatives. They built a library, built or improved about one hundred homes, and installed a village sewer system. They also constructed three miles of road and negotiated a new bus service. They trained local paramedics and built and staffed a medical/dental clinic in addition to setting up a comprehensive public health program that included vaccinations, prenatal care, and nutrition and health education.

Action projects such as well drilling in Tinaja, Mexico, bring a community visible dividends as well as the long-term benefits of new information, skills, and attitudes.

Sixty miles to the north, in Santa Rosa, a remote village much like Tinaja, stands another clinic building. Unlike Tinaja's structure, this center was conceived, financed, and built by outsiders—university and government officials. Santa Rosa's facility has a fancier design than Tinaja's clinic and cost twice as much to build.

The grand Santa Rosa clinic is abandoned. The people were not involved in the decision to build it. It wasn't theirs. The officials who commissioned the building were very well intentioned. They saw critical health needs in the community, but didn't know how to include the local people in planning and directing the solution. By beginning with the technical and capital elements of the project, rather than the human aspects, they ended up spending too much for the latest and the best facilities. The outsiders ran out of money and commitment. The clinic was never completed. Its unfinished roof rots in the weather. The people of Santa Rosa are now starting their own literacy-for-social-change program. In the context of their new goals for learning and action, they may yet take ownership of the building project. Only they can make the clinic a viable community resource.

Each successive action project in the Tinaja experiment was based upon participant needs and goals. Clinics and wells may be visible dividends of this learning process, but long-term payoff is best measured in the new information, skills, and attitudes achieved by the people. These are more permanent outcomes that will benefit the community for generations to come.

Like Tinaja, other literacy-for-social-change efforts bring about impressive project achievements. Tabasará, Panama, literacy learners have planted community gardens, established a cooperative store, and improved their homes. Rural learners in Lanao, Philippines, have developed a cooperative for selling fish. Women in Dhaka, Bangladesh, now weave and sell their goods on a cooperative basis. Slum dwellers outside Port-au-Prince, Haiti, have established a poultry cooperative and public health program. Inner-city learners in Watts (south central Los Angeles) have established a private school for their children and a neighborhood cultural program. South Pasadena, California, adult learners have set up a neighborhood recreation and health/cultural education program. Literacy learners in Kerala, India, produce and sell clothing. Women near Chiang Mai, Thailand, have established an agricultural enterprise. Landless men near Cavite, Philippines, now harvest rice on a cooperative basis. Mothers in Calamar, Colombia, have built a small health clinic by hand. Learners in Medellín's former garbage dump have constructed hundreds of brick homes where shacks once stood.

Don't try to separate literacy and development.

Leaders who are committed to a participant-generated development process often fail to make the connection between literacy and development. Reading and writing education needn't be a process separate from the development aspirations of the people. In fact, the two profoundly enhance each other. As people gain greater mastery over the language of their lives, they acquire greater capacity and confidence to initiate and maintain needed community and individual change. Moreover, people have far greater motivation to learn when convinced that the learning is directly connected to the resolution of problems in their lives.

As Dr. Luís Oscar Londoño has put it, from the outset every literacy program should have a community development component with specific action projects, and conversely every community development effort should have a literacy and education starting point. In neighborhoods and villages where literacy skill levels are varied, more skilled learners often can help the others. At times they can meet with their own skill-level groups and at other times work as a total community. For real success, literacy and community development belong together.

Criteria for selecting action projects

Outside funds and leadership aimed at a physical need defined by outsiders rarely result in lasting grassroots development. But a program that integrates fundamental skills, cultural expression, critical thinking, and action projects within the context of participant goals and aspirations can bring about permanent change. With this integrated approach in mind, the action projects that do receive the finite time, energy, and resources of the participants and funding sources should be very carefully selected. The following five criteria are crucial.

1. The project should be selected by the participants. Outsiders may interact with this decision-making process, but the final decision should come from the people. People won't give the necessary time and energy to complete the project if they aren't totally convinced that the project meets their own goals.

Ideally, that decision and commitment will flow from the dialogue and problem posing of the literacy learning experience.

2. The project should have an identifiable learning "curriculum" that enables participants to apply existing skills and to acquire new skills, information, and perspectives.
3. The project's implementation should stimulate new social and economic relationships that empower participants with a greater degree of self-determination. Too much money contributed from the outside, while temporarily helpful, may create harmful dependence.
4. Outside agencies may introduce seed money or technical help to get the effort started, but the participants also need to invest their own time, work, and possibly money to implement the project. The project needs to become locally self-sustaining and independent of outside donations.
5. The project should meet specific needs of participants, such as health, potable water, or income generation. If income generation is the project's primary goal, then the earnings should not only be distributed among the participants and/or reinvested in the project, but some amount should be invested to meet broader community needs identified by the people.

Literacy for social change—the process that integrates basic skills, critical thinking, cultural expression, and action projects—is a model for community development. The how-to steps and underlying concepts described throughout this book apply to development as well as education. Without education, genuine development is impossible. And effective development generates education.

The successful development leader is therefore a successful facilitator of learning. Action projects demand active follow-up, and leadership committed to the people. That leadership is effective if it enables participants to develop their own capacity to lead. Local leadership and organizational development are critical elements of success.

A development worker from Bolivia described one essential characteristic of a literacy-for-social-change leader. "She has to be committed with her heart. When the people have evidence over time that she really cares, they'll trust her. That kind of trust motivates others to become leaders and generates a spirit of unity and enthusiasm that grows in the village. Without this solidarity, the project will die away."

Similarly, Frank C. Laubach, founder of Laubach Literacy International, once observed that effective literacy projects create many "silver threads of love" that bind the effort together and inspire ever greater levels of commitment and action.

Technical learning is also important. In the same way that basic reading skill instruction can be integrated into the dialogue experience, lessons on the technology of a given project can also be integrated into the process. As long as facilitators remember the principle—*Start (and end) with the learners*—then new ideas and technologies can be introduced and explained within the context of participant issues and culture.

Part IV
Implications

Chapter 11

Overcoming obstacles and measuring success

Literacy education is saturated with politics. Even those who think they are just helping another human being to learn are involved in a very political act. Every individual who learns to read and write has acquired skills that can help sustain the established social, economic, and political order—or perhaps oppose it. Either way, the implications are political. New readers can become more supportive, loyal citizens and they can help society be more productive. But literacy education can also empower people to demand their legal rights, express their legitimate concerns, resist injustices in their communities, and create a better life for themselves and their neighbors. Such activities don't necessarily find favor with those who control some aspect of learners' lives.

Active programs, particularly among the poor, can generate opposition. Reading students in Chicago who learned how to obtain fair credit rates infuriated local loan sharks who plagued their inner-city neighborhood. A Colombian factory sponsored a literacy class for its employees, but balked when workers learned to read bulletin-board notices about Colombia's legal minimum wage. The workers asked why they didn't receive the minimum wage and were all promptly fired. Some husbands in Philadelphia harassed or assaulted their spouses for participating in literacy discussions on the legal rights of abused wives and children.

One of the first words Bangladesh farm workers learn in a rural literacy program is the Bengali term which means "to be cheated." They then learn math skills to get a fair deal at the marketplace and, in the process, anger powerful traders who no longer make such exploitatively high profits. In Haiti, a literacy student "disappeared" at the hands of police, and the program director went into hiding. The director's name appeared on a death list because newly literate learners in his classes could now read the ballot and refused to sell their votes to the government candidate.

Government officials, police, landowners, and powerful business owners sometimes resist the literacy efforts of poorer people in their area. This opposition generally takes the form of mild administrative or organizational harassment, but indigenous literacy workers in various countries have on occasion been stripped and searched, beaten, kidnapped, harassed, shot, or robbed by the police or hired vigilantes.

Opposition to effective literacy programs can be very real. Fortunately, it doesn't usually reach the life-threatening stage. But it can present an intimidating challenge for those committed to literacy at the grassroots level.

From 1982 to 1986, I conducted dissertation research involving unstructured interviews with forty-two literacy facilitators and twenty-six learners from programs inside and outside the United States. These programs were all located in lower-income neighborhoods and villages and all attempted to emphasize learner-guided and bicultural educational approaches. Respondents repeatedly described their work as a struggle characterized by intense personal and programmatic reward and equally intense opposition. The opposition results from many factors, all of which are linked to the political realities inherent when a program attempts to incorporate the perspective of a disenfranchised learner population.

The scores of literacy activists working among the poor whom I interviewed are deeply committed to the ideal of literacy for social change. In varying degrees their commitment is reflected in their practice. But all of them report that their practice falls short of their vision. They have to negotiate a range of compromises to keep the greater portion of their ideal alive. In the face of opposition and misunderstanding, they struggle, sacrifice, find creative alternatives, and sometimes make painful trade-offs.

Obstacles

Leaders involved in literacy-for-social-change programs often encounter the following obstacles:

Lack of resources. This is the biggest problem. Few funding sources share their broader vision of literacy. Many of the best programs are struggling to stay alive.

Difficulty in defining and conveying success. Too many people judge program success solely on mastery of basic reading and writing skills. The other significant achievements of the program are often missed.

Difficulty maintaining clarity and continuity. A learner-guided, holistic process sometimes wanders and takes unexpected directions.

Professional risk. For leaders of such programs, employment security, professional status, and income levels are often uncertain. It can be a tough career field.

Physical discomfort and danger. Either or both can be part of the experience.

Cultural disorientation and a sense of isolation. Leaders are often caught in the uncomfortable middle between two cultural worlds—their own and that of the learners.

Emotional stress. Leaders sometimes find it difficult to reconcile working with the poor without being poor themselves. Their emotional involvement may lead to strain on family life, frustration, and burnout.

Several leaders have adapted pragmatic perspectives to accommodate the reality of a world preoccupied with a very narrow notion of literacy education. That pragmatism often involves compromise. But carefully conceived trade-offs can maximize success and minimize the losses. In spite of the opposition, there is ample evidence for hope and perseverance.

Street-tough learners from Bronx Educational Services in New York City felt intimidated by the prospect of foundation fund-raising. With encouragement and support, they succeeded in obtaining corporate funds when they presented their literacy program to Manhattan executives. Bolivian peasants conducted a literacy program with no meeting facilities, but their persistence and enthusiasm attracted government support to help them build a community learning center. A central California program overcame county resistance to establish a successful bilingual program among migrant workers.

When officials in a small town outside Kathmandu, Nepal, harassed women literacy learners by padlocking the classroom and arresting the instructor, participants went door-to-door to generate citizen support, and arranged for the release of their teacher and the reinstatement of the program with town funds. In Syracuse, New York, persistent volunteers at The Learning Place secured building space and community donations in spite of people's initial lack of interest.

The assassination of a student by landowners who opposed a rural Colombian literacy program not only failed to intimidate the other learners but became a rallying point for widespread community support. Today the program is thriving.

Effective evaluation

Committed leaders, learners, and advocates of literacy for social change can overcome opposition and win support and resources for their programs. Perseverance and enthusiasm are essential, but to enable others to support the effort, leaders also need to convey a clear picture of what constitutes success. People are more likely to support a program if they can see its positive results. Effective evaluation should not only enable planners and participants to document and "sell" a program's achievements, but to help identify areas of needed improvement and growth.

Each program needs to identify its own measures of success. Participants of the former *Barrio* Education Project in San Antonio, Texas, were asked to evaluate their educational experience. Each person was asked to rank the ten most important things they had learned from the community-oriented program. Their responses were both surprising and revealing.

Program leaders already knew that the participants had made dramatic gains in reading and writing skills; this was, after all, a literacy project. They therefore expected learners to put reading and writing basics at the top of their lists. But participants viewed their experience from a very different perspective. Learning to read and write appeared on everybody's page, but on the average it was ranked eighth or ninth in priority.

High on the list were unexpected outcomes. "I saw that I could make new friends." "I found out more about our community." "We talked about important problems." "We worked together." "We sang together." Program evaluators could have dismissed these options as student misunderstanding of what is important. Instead, based on this input from learners, leaders reassessed the goals of the program to incorporate these unanticipated results into the educational process. Actually, learners were describing outcomes that included critical thinking and cultural expression.

A conventional indicator of a literacy program's success involves students' pre- and post-test scores for basic reading and writing. In the San Antonio project, such tests may have shown that the program was adequate, but they would have missed the program's other significant accomplishments. Evaluation can't be limited to tests.

Funders and policy makers, although calling increasingly for greater accountability, are rarely equipped to look at the whole range of achievements. This reality poses a challenge for all. To assure survival, program leaders need to present their programs attractively without compromising their neighborhood-based character. Funders and policy makers need to relax some of the superficial and bureaucratic requirements that exclude effective grassroots programs.

For many reasons, program leaders, planners, evaluators, and prospective funders need to look at the genuine achievements and potential of community literacy programs. Such a focus keeps programs true to their first constituency, the learners. With such an orientation, evaluation becomes first and foremost a tool for planning and for program improvement.

Many grassroots literacy programs approach learning in terms of the total life context of the learner. Such programs should be evaluated in the same terms. Learners should play a major role in defining and measuring success. Testing measurements may be helpful, but uniform learning outcomes should not be expected.

No two programs that emphasize learner-guided and bicultural approaches are likely to be the same. Their connection to the broader concerns of their respective community settings creates unique program outcomes. Each program may evolve beyond a specific focus on reading and writing to encompass community development, celebration of culture, and political dialogue/action, along with a wide range of subjects of interest to learners.

The most important measures of success in these programs are not necessarily seen immediately. New perspectives and attitudes arising from the learning process can generate a deep and lasting base for ongoing individual and social change, but these changes generally take years to be manifested. Real success for individual learners will be reflected in such long-term indicators as success in negotiating with agencies and vendors with whom the learners had previously experienced failure; improved management of family resources; improved employment and income; enrollment in further educational programs; and more active participation in children's schooling, study groups, or other community activities. Long-term indicators of group success include community changes such as cooperative income-generation activities, community development projects, cultural celebration initiatives, and implementation of political/social change in response to locally identified needs.

The long-term measures of program success may take years to emerge, but many immediate, concrete results of the learning process are predictors of more profound and lasting change. A useful evaluation seeks to describe and acknowledge the meaningful things that occur. Some behavioral outcomes are desirable. Performances in these areas can and should be measured. But the most accurate sources of information are the people who are experiencing the process. And they probably won't describe their achievements in the format or terms that funding sources expect to deal with. Funders may need to learn to think in more holistic terms so that they can comprehend what is truly happening.

Program leaders, on the other hand, can help report learner achievements in terms that funders are more comfortable hearing. They can describe several of the early indicators of success. The specific experience of a given program will suggest which indicators are most useful. Standardized test scores may still have value, but the following examples suggest a much broader range of possibilities.

Sample learning indicators

1. Participation in group discussion activities.
2. Increasing proficiency in describing and analyzing complex concepts.
3. Proficiency in stating the relationship of other learners' concerns to the learner's own concerns.
4. Expanding circle of interest and activity beyond the more local, immediate level to regional, national, and even international levels.
5. Analysis of problems that extends beyond the immediate present to include historical and future aspects.
6. Use of printed materials to gain information to solve problems. Descriptions of the new ways in which learners have been able to solve problems.
7. Use of reading and writing in group learning sessions.
8. Letters, stories, or other items written by the learners.
9. Descriptions of activities that illustrate a new capacity in areas such as decision making, goal setting, management, interpersonal relationships, and parenting.

10. Demonstrations or descriptions of achievement in areas such as hygiene, music, animal care, marketing, art, drama, dance, and cooking.

How would this learner in a Bangladesh literacy class describe her achievements?

One very useful tool for setting objectives is the learning contract. A learning contract is simply an agreement, often written, between the learners and facilitators about what will be accomplished during the learning experience. If learners initiate the contract, they can state objectives for their learning experience and commit themselves to attaining these objectives. Such agreements can also include a commitment to attendance and individual study, and spell out what the program will offer in return. The development of the learning contract is in itself a learning activity.

During the course of learning, and certainly at the end of a targeted time period, learners and leaders can use the contract objectives as a useful tool for reflection and evaluation. Were objectives achieved? How did the learning take place? Why weren't some objectives realized? Where do we go from here?

Even with learning objectives stated, a successful learner-guided process will undoubtedly stimulate new objectives and possibilities along the way. Flexibility, even in the most meticulously planned learning effort, is a necessity.

Chapter 12

Where to go from here?

Not every literacy organization is voicing concern about how to reach unserved audiences, but many are. Serving new populations requires new approaches, attitudes, and partnerships to get the job done.

A few years ago, the Columbus, Ohio, Literacy Council, a one-to-one volunteer tutoring program, identified issues that many other literacy organizations throughout the United States and in other parts of the world continue to raise. Why isn't our program serving more of the hard-to-reach potential learners? Why aren't we succeeding in inner-city neighborhoods with minority population groups? Their serious discussion of these questions led them to consider new partners and methods to address the unmet need. Some of their leaders expressed concern that such changes might undermine the effective base already established. After discussion and debate, they concluded that some new thrusts were possible and desirable. But to preserve unity within the program, those who remained in the program's traditional teaching format and those who became involved in new efforts would have to maintain an active mutual respect.

The Columbus program initiated student conversation groups for peer support and dialogue. They also began working with an existing black neighborhood organization. Their experiment yielded a number of failures and rewards. Two years after they began, they reported limited but growing success in an effort to work effectively with groups previously unserved. The organization has also expanded its traditional one-to-one tutoring program, and the mutual respect of the groups has been maintained. Such mutual affirmation is an important element in the success of both.

Generally, existing programs that experiment with meaningful ways to serve new audiences are in a state of transition. A southern California group invites learners to participate in "learning circle" dialogue groups one day a week. The learners meet in standard one-to-one tutoring on another day of the week. Project WILL (Women in Laubach Literacy) in Pine Bluff, Arkansas, transports young inner-city mothers to the Pine Bluff campus of the University of Arkansas for a session of one-to-one tutoring followed by a group activity in the areas of problem solving, peer support, parenting skills, and writing. Their children receive day care and take part in a preschool program at a nearby Baptist church.

Book clubs for learner reading and discussion, student support groups, and discussion circles all combine dialogue groups with conventional tutoring or classroom instruction. Teachers and tutors in conventional programs often insert curriculum and learning activities that focus on learner culture, issues, and dialogue, even on a one-to-one basis. A number of programs have located in inner-city churches, neighborhood centers, and storefront learning sites in order to position literacy classes close to the learners' homes. Mainstream organizations have joined with Indian reservations, migrant organizations, *barrio* groups, ethnic cultural programs, tenant unions, and other special populations to establish literacy programs within community settings. Often, ethnic neighborhood groups create their own community-based programs, but get training and materials from traditional outside sources.

Programs and individuals initiating such steps for improvement frequently report success and satisfaction in working with previously unserved learners. In the process, they are also forced to deal with sometimes unsettling cultural and organizational changes. Scholars, opinion leaders, development workers, or concerned community participants will probably confront similar difficulties in their efforts at advocacy or program change. In spite of the challenge, however, the attempt is clearly well worth the effort.

The literacy-for-social-change model works, especially among disenfranchised populations who tend to be bypassed by traditional education and development efforts. It responds to a definition of literacy that can enable people to solve problems, take advantage of the opportunities in their environment, and participate in the transformation of their society. Because it recognizes that literacy is one thread in a complex social and political fabric, it seeks to integrate basic skills, critical thinking, cultural expression, and action as a practical way of achieving its goal: a just and equitable society.

Transformations don't come easily, for society, for organizations, or for individuals. Change may begin with small steps, however, that lead to bigger ones. Those who see the value of the literacy-for-social-change model, but who might not be prepared to take immediate, specific action, might start by considering one of the suggestions in the following list. It includes possibilities ranging from increasing sensitivity to marginalized learner groups, to program-specific activities. Not all the suggestions will apply to everyone, but perhaps one or two will trigger further response.

Develop awareness.

1. Research living conditions of a local ethnic minority group.
2. Visit a shelter for the homeless with co-workers.
3. Take a walk in the inner city and get to know five residents.
4. Read a book on Indian culture by a Native American author.
5. Discuss the causes of poverty in your community.
6. Learn the words of the Black National Anthem.
7. Discuss the heroes of the Mexican Revolution.
8. Discuss the impact of hunger and deforestation on the poor.
9. Write down your own definition of literacy.
10. Discuss the roles of women in literacy and community development.
11. List the benefits of dialogue as a vehicle for literacy learning.

Create learning opportunities.

12. Write a reading lesson based upon interviews with learners.
13. Develop a skit about village health issues.
14. Compose a simple story about housing issues.
15. Develop opportunities for peer tutoring to take place.
16. Plant a community garden with your learning group.

17. Experiment with one of the techniques suggested in chapter 7.
18. Help literacy students form a learner support and dialogue group.
19. Assist learners to document a neighborhood issue through photos.
20. Invite learners to evaluate their learning experience.

Initiate program changes.

21. Invite learners to serve on your board.
22. State the first goal of your literacy program. Should it change?
23. Insist that development projects have a literacy component.
24. Urge staff to identify grassroots organizations for joint work.
25. Ask your board, "Why aren't we working in the inner city?"
26. *Start with the learners!*

Select bibliography

ACBE. 1983. *Standards of performance for community-based educational institutions, Self-assessment workbook.* Washington, DC: Association for Community Based Education.

ACBE. 1989. *Literacy for empowerment: A resource handbook.* Washington, DC: Association for Community Based Education.

Adams, F., and M. Horton. 1980. *Unearthing seeds of fire.* Winston-Salem, NC: John F. Blair.

Anderson, D., and J.A. Niemi. 1970. *Adult education and the disadvantaged adult.* Syracuse, NY: Syracuse University Publications in Continuing Education.

Armstrong, A.K. 1977. *Masters of their own destiny: A comparison of the thought of Coady and Freire.* Vancouver, British Columbia: University of British Columbia.

BCEL. 1984, September. Community-based organizations: Reaching the hardest-to-reach. *Business Council for Effective Literacy: A Newsletter for the Business Community.* (New York: Business Council for Effective Literacy).

Bilingual Education Office, California State Department of Education. 1986. *Beyond language: Social and cultural factors in schooling language minority students.* Los Angeles, CA: Evaluation, Dissemination, and Assessment Center, California State University.

Brown, C. 1974, July-August. Literacy in thirty hours: Paulo Freire's process in northeast Brazil. *Social Policy.* (New York: Social Policy Corporation).

Bunder, R. 1985. *Two ears of corn: A guide to people-centered agricultural improvement.* Oklahoma City, OK: World Neighbors.

Cadena, F. 1984. Popular adult education and peasant movements for social change. *Convergence.* (Toronto: International Council for Adult Education) 17 (3): 31-36.

Carpenter, T. 1986. *Tutor's handbook for the SCIL (Student Centered Individualized Learning) program.* Toronto: Frontier College.

Comings, J.P., and D. Kahler. 1984. *Peace Corps literacy handbook.* Washington, DC: Peace Corps.

Coover, V., E. Deacon, C. Esser, and C. Moore. 1978. *Resource manual for a living revolution.* Philadelphia, PA: New Society Publishers.

Crone, C.D., and C. St. J. Hunter. 1980. *From the field: Tested participatory activities for trainers.* New York: World Education.

Facundo, B. 1984. *Issues for an evaluation of Freire-inspired programs in the United States and Puerto Rico.* Rio Piedras, Puerto Rico: Alternatives.

Fingeret, A., and P. Jurmo. 1989. *Participatory literacy education.* New Directions for Continuing Education Series. San Francisco, CA: Jossey-Bass, Inc. Publishers.

Freire, P. 1970. *Pedagogy of the oppressed.* New York: Seabury Press.

Freire, P. 1973. *Education for critical consciousness.* New York: Seabury Press.

Freire, P. 1978. *Pedagogy in process: Letters to Guinea-Bissau.* New York: Seabury Press.

Freire, P. 1985. *The politics of education: Culture, power, and liberation.* South Hadley, MA: Bergin and Gorvey Publishers, Inc.

Freire, P. 1987. *Reading the word and the world.* South Hadley, MA: Bergin and Gorvey Publishers, Inc.

Grabowski, S., ed. 1972. *Paulo Freire: A revolutionary dilemma for the adult educator.* Syracuse, NY: ERIC Clearinghouse on Adult Education.

Halperin, S. 1981. *A guide for the powerless and those who don't know their own power.* Washington, DC: The Institute for Educational Leadership.

Harman, D. 1985. *Turning illiteracy around: An agenda for national action: Working paper no. 2.* New York: Business Council for Effective Literacy.

Harman, D. 1987. *Illiteracy: A national dilemma.* New York: Cambridge.

Heaney, T.W. 1984. *Struggling to be free: The story of universidad popular.* Fund for the Improvement of Postsecondary Education. (ERIC Document Reproduction Service No. ED 241677).

Hirshon, S. 1983. *And also teach them to read.* Westport, CT: Lawrence Hill and Co.

Horton, M. 1966, May. It's a miracle—I still don't believe it. (interview). *Phi Delta Kappan.* (Bloomington, IN: Phi Delta Kappa, Inc.).

Hoyles, M., ed. 1977. *The politics of literacy.* London, England: Writers and Readers Publishing Cooperative.

Hunger Project, The. 1985. *Ending hunger: An idea whose time has come.* New York: Praeger.

Hunter, C. St. J., and D. Harman. 1979. *Adult literacy in the United States.* New York: McGraw-Hill Book Company.

Ilsley, P. 1985. *Adult literacy volunteers: Issues and ideas.* Columbus, OH: ERIC Clearinghouse on Adult, Career, and Vocational Education. The National Center for Research in Vocational Education, Ohio State University.

Jakes, C.L., and R.F. Caswell. 1974. *Libros para neolectores.* Syracuse, NY: Laubach Literacy International.

James, M. 1990. Demystifying literacy: Reading, writing, and the struggle for liberation. *Convergence.* (Toronto: International Council for Adult Education) 23 (1): 14-26.

Kalmar, T.M. 1983. *The voice of Fulano: Working papers from a bilingual literacy campaign.* Cambridge, MA: Schenkman Publishing Co.

Korten, D.C., and R. Klauss, eds. 1984. *People-centered development: Contributions toward theory and planning frameworks.* West Hartford, CT: Kumarian Press.

Kozol, J. 1980. *Prisoners of silence.* New York: Continuum Publishing.

Kozol, J. 1985. *Illiterate America.* Garden City, NJ: Anchor Press/ Doubleday.

Lankshear, C., and M. Lawler. 1987. *Literacy, schooling, and revolution.* Philadelphia, PA: The Falmer Press, Taylor and Francis, Inc.

Laubach, F.C. 1945. *The silent billion speak.* New York: Friendship Press.

Luttrell, W. 1982. *Building multi-cultural awareness: A teaching approach for learner-centered education.* Philadelphia, PA: Lutheran Settlement House.

Mackie, R., ed. 1981. *Literacy and revolution: The pedagogy of Paulo Freire.* New York: The Continuum Publishing Co.

National Dissemination Study Group, The. 1989. *Educational practices that work: A collection of proven exemplary educational programs and practices.* Longmont, CO: Sopris West, Inc.

Noble, P. 1983. *Formation of Freirian facilitators.* Chicago, IL: Latino Institute.

Piedrahita, H. 1982. *Historica de un barrio de invasion.* Medellín, Colombia: Centro Laubach de Educación Popular Básica de Adultos.

Quinones, A.B., and J. Cook. 1983. *Spanish literacy investigation project.* New York: Solidaridad Humana.

Reder, S.M. 1985. *Giving literacy away. Alternative strategies for increasing adult literacy development, training capacity, and program participation.* San Francisco, CA: National Adult Literacy Project, Far West Laboratory for Educational Research and Development. Andover, MA: The NETWORK. (ERIC Document Reproduction Service No. ED 253775).

Shor, I., ed. 1987. *Freire for the classroom: A sourcebook for liberatory teaching.* Boynton/Cook Publishers.

Shor, I., and P. Freire. 1987. *A pedagogy for liberation: Dialogues for transforming education.* Bergin Publishers, Inc.

Svendson, D.S., and S. Wijetilleke. 1983. *Navamanga: Training activities for group building.* Washington, DC: Overseas Development Fund.

Vella, J.K. 1979. *Learning to listen: A guide to methods of adult nonformal education.* Amherst, MA: Center for International Education.

Wallerstein, N. 1982. *Language and culture in conflict*. Reading, MA: Addison-Wesley Publishing Co.

Werner, D., and B. Bower. 1982. *Helping health workers learn*. Palo Alto, CA: Hesperian Foundation.

Women's Self-Help Network. 1984. *Working together for change*. Courtenay, British Columbia, Canada: North Island Woman's Services Society.

Zachariadis, C. 1986. *Adult literacy: A study of community-based literacy programs*. Washington, DC: Association for Community Based Education.

Index

A

B

C

R

S

T

U

V

W

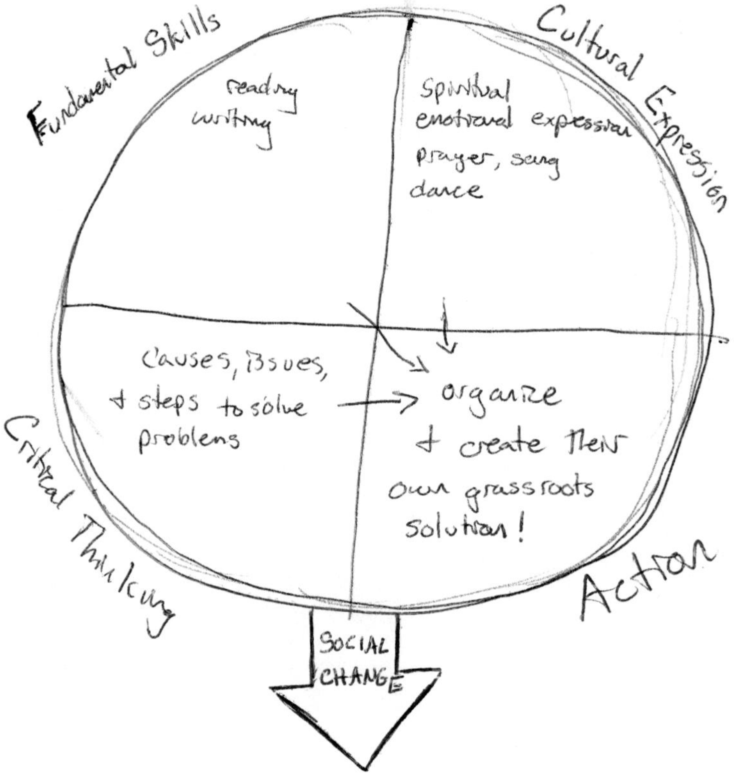

Fundamental Skills

reading
writing

Cultural Expression

spiritual
emotional expression
prayer, song
dance

Critical Thinking

Causes, issues,
+ steps to solve
problems

Action

organize
+ create their
own grassroots
solution!

SOCIAL
CHANGE

CODE'S - pictures, depict reality for learners

words become codes for issues/experiences that the people face daily and feel strongly about.